THE DREAMER

Dave Brett

The Dreamer

Copyright © Dave Brett 2024
www.davebrett.co.uk

All rights reserved. This book or parts thereof may not be reproduced in any form, stored in any retrieval system, or transmitted in any form by any means—electronic, mechanical, photocopy, recording, or otherwise—without prior written permission of the publisher. For permission requests, write to the publisher, at admin@davebrett.co.uk All rights reserved.

Dedication

This book is dedicated to the young girl who became my inspiration, she beat cancer's backside! But pneumonia and septicaemia were just too much. She died a hero to so many.
Ellie-Morgan Sasha Abbey
RIP 2003-2016

Contents

ACKNOWLEDGEMENTS 1

THE DARK AND LONELY ROAD 3

EUREKA 18

LONDON'S CALLING 28

JUST GO FOR IT 44

BACK TO REALITY 54

ALL GO AND NO SHOW 60

TO THE RESCUE 72

IF AT FIRST YOU DON'T SUCCEED 77

A DIFFERENT WORLD 83

MOMENT OF TRUTH 87

LIVING THE DREAM 94

STRIVING FOR SUCCESS AGAINST ALL THE ODDS 103

QUIET PEOPLE HAVE THE LOUDEST MINDS 116

THE PINNACLE OF MY LIFE 123

STARS CAN'T SHINE WITHOUT DARKNESS 140

THE NEXT CHAPTER 149

INSPIRATIONAL QUOTES 152

Acknowledgements

I would just like to thank all the people I have worked with in recruitment and placed into work, I thank you all for putting your trust in me.

I would like to thank everyone who helped me along the way. The help you provided was essential and every business needs people to guide you and support you along the way. Thank you to all my family and friends for your amazing support when I needed it the most.

And thank you, the reader, for purchasing this book, I hope you enjoy it and maybe even pick up some helpful advice and tips I picked up along the way. But please bear in mind, this isn't a "how to start a business" book. This book is my story and I hope to inspire or encourage others to try and reach out to grasp your dreams.

The Dark and Lonely Road

It was a cold evening, and I was sitting in the passenger seat of a lorry on the way home to Cliftonville, my clothes and steel toe cap boots covered in mud. I would wear my old clothes to work. These were often grey joggers and an ancient blue New York Yankees hoody, with so many holes in them they looked like rags. Tonight, at the end of another twelve-hour gruelling shift, my body was in ruins.

The motorway lights flashed an orange light in the lorry's cab as I desperately tried to keep my eyes open. It was late in the year so the night began so much earlier. I remember looking at my hands that were split open from carrying kerbs all day. It made me worry as I was climbing down sewers and repairing pipes every day as well. Would my hands get infected? I was self-employed at the time and if I couldn't use my hands I was out of work, which meant no money.

I was 23 years old, deep in debt and just living from day to day, quickly taking my wages out in cash at the ATM before debtors could get it. I was staying at a random person's house who had a spare room; her name was Margaret. My mate had told me about her place. It was just to tide me over until I could afford a flat of my own. Located on the outskirts of town, my tiny room contained a single bed and a sink. I shared the bathroom with Margaret and her other two lodgers.

Margaret was a ruthless businesswoman. She had owned a B&B in Cliftonville in its heyday when the tourist trade there was booming and money was pouring into it. But when seaside towns in the area fell from grace just after the millennium, unable to compete with cheap package holidays abroad, she was forced to sell up and rent out parts of her house to strangers.

I was two months behind on rent. When I wasn't working because work had dried up, I hid myself away, locking the door of my room, pretending I was asleep when she knocked. It was always an awkward dodge getting into the house; I'd try to open the front door ever so quietly to then run up the stairs without being noticed and avoid confrontation.

The lorry was too big to be driven down the narrow road to my place, so it dropped me off at the end of the road. I jumped from the very tall cab and instantly felt the bitter cold. I just wanted to quickly get inside and get warm.

As I walked towards the dreaded house, I could see bags outside the front door. As I edged closer I could see a black bin liner and my rucksack. It seemed Margaret had finally given up with me.

I looked at my belongings. I could see a note, "Don't bother knocking, we don't want to hear any more excuses, we just want you gone."

I looked up at the house; all the lights were off. It reminded me of Halloween when you knock on a door and you know someone is in, but they have all the lights off and are trying to pretend no one's home. What could I do? I didn't have a lease. Margaret had agreed to me staying with a handshake. I should have been expecting this.

Inside the black bin liner were some of my clothes, trainers and a few other belongings. My rucksack contained my phone charger and some spare work clothes. Which again were old rags with holes in, but at least these were semi-clean rags with holes in. You could never get the smell of tarmac and diesel out of my work clothes; this was always a problem when I wanted to wash my clothes. Margaret had hated me using her washing machine to wash my clothes.

"Can't you go down the launderette? No offence, but I don't want my clothes to smell like a building site!"

To be honest, I could see her point a bit.

I picked up my rucksack and put it on my back. The bin bag I just left. It contained things that could be replaced, at some point. I turned and looked at the dark road dimly lit by the orange streetlight.

Where do I go now? I hadn't seen or spoken to my parents in

The Dark and Lonely Road

years. Pride wouldn't let me call them; I was too ashamed to go there. Especially given the state I looked. Luckily, before I jumped out of the lorry, I grabbed my hi-vis bomber jacket, but just like the rest of my work clothes it was filthy and ripped, but at least it kept some of the cold at bay.

I began walking up the narrow street and headed towards the nearest town centre. I pulled my Samsung Galaxy Mini out of my pocket. Because I was so bad with money no contract company would touch me, so I was using pay-as-you-go. The battery cover was missing and the phone was smashed and broken, being held together with Sellotape.

I clicked on the centre button, the screen lit up my face and I clicked on my contacts list, scrolling through trying to find a friend who would put me up for the night. I didn't really have a lot of friends, so it didn't take me very long to go through the list. I texted two mates who were in nearby Margate. I wasn't very hopeful of a reply, but if they did get back to me, they were within walking distance.

As I walked towards the main high street in Cliftonville I started to feel very vulnerable because of the groups of people hanging around on corners. Shops boarded up, rubbish left everywhere, and you just felt at any minute you would be jumped. You would always see some random discarded fridge or chest freezer left on the footpath.

Where was I going to stay tonight? I pulled my phone out of my pocket hoping I would see '1 new message', desperate for one of my only friends to help me out. But it was an empty screen. I had known one of them for fifteen years... some friend.

What was I going to do now? I had a girlfriend, Laura, but it was always on and off and she lived in London which was at least a two-and-a-half-hour train ride away. But I couldn't just leave my only source of income and go to London. Besides, she lived with her auntie and I very much doubted they would let me stay without a job

The Dreamer

and riddled with debt collectors chasing after me.

Laura was beautiful. She used to live in Thanet. That's where I'd met her. With her blondish-brown hair, she was the spitting image of Kate Winslet in Titanic. It's hard to maintain a relationship long-distance, and when we did meet up, despite wanting to live together, our arguments were often about not having the money to make that move. Her job was on the tills at Tesco, and although it was a steady job, we simply couldn't afford to get our own place. This made me feel really unhappy. Laura wanted the perfect family life and I was desperate to give it to her; a house with a mortgage, a nice car on the drive, a big back garden for her dog to run free and just to be able to live a free life without having other peoples' rules imposed on us. Would we ever be in a position to do this, I often wondered.

I finally walked to an ATM that wasn't surrounded by people. I had no idea how much money was in my account. As I entered my pin I started hoping I might just have enough to get a bed and breakfast for the night. My balance then came up on screen: £56 overdrawn, and I didn't even have an overdraft agreement.

I was paid weekly, and on Fridays I quickly withdrew all the cash I could before debtors could take it, but the bank had already allowed a payment to go out. Everyone knows that payday loans are a terrible deal, but what are you supposed to do if it's the only option available to you, and at this point I only ever had enough money to pay off the last fee, never the loan itself, which just kept escalating. This had now taken me into an unarranged overdraft. This meant even more trouble with the bank. I knew I would now be charged for this and interest per day.

As I withdrew my card I could see the ATM displaying '£2.50 withdrawal charge'. I didn't even have that in my account!

I pulled out my wallet and saw £20. My last £20, this was all the money I had in the world. What the hell was I going to be able to get with that? There wasn't a bed and breakfast around here that would put me up for £20.

The Dark and Lonely Road

The ATM was in an off-licence window. Just to the right was a notice board with all sorts of advertisements. In the bottom corner I saw 'bed and breakfast, good rates and tradesmen welcome'. I had stayed there once before; I knew it was cheap and very nice. I phoned the number, "How much for a room tonight please?"

"£40" came the voice.

"Would you take £20? It's all I've got. I'm desperate. I've stayed with you before."

"Alright mate. Call it £30. That's as low as I can go."

I was still £10 down. After telling him I would be there shortly, I put down the phone and then began panicking about how I would get the extra £10. In the distance I saw a betting shop, the lights were on and other than a few kebab shops and pizza places it was the only thing open.

Walking towards the bookies I pondered on what I was about to do. I was about to risk all the money I had to get a room for the night. If this didn't work it would be a night on the nearest bench and that would be a very cold night. I had my hands clenched in my bomber jacket pocket just trying to keep them warm.

As I opened the door the bookies was completely empty. The cashier behind the desk was waiting to close for the night. Across the floor there was a betting machine, roulette was the game of choice. Pulling the £20 from my wallet and hearing the sound of the machine sucking it in, my heart raced. '£20 cash' then came up on the corner of the screen. Should I put it all on, or just some? Hesitantly I put chips on the electronic board, ten pence here, twenty pence there, then I would erase the whole thing and start again. Red or black seemed the only option.

£5 on black. If it won, I'd just need one more win and I'd have enough. The wheel spun and landed on red! The balance now read £15.

The only way to get to £30 now was to just risk it all. £15 on red! The ball spun around for what felt like an eternity! Then I heard the words...... FOURTEEN RED!

The cash balance now read £30! I quickly pushed the cash button and waited impatiently for my ticket to be printed, and when it did, I ran it to the cashier to get the money for a nice warm bed.

I walked towards Margate seafront where the B&B was, it was along the coastal road. This route took me alongside the beach and I could see out into the endless darkness of the sea. The sea was very rough and the whites of the waves crashed against the beach. The wind was picking up even more now. But at least in the distance I could see my dimly lit B&B. I knocked on the door and gave the owner my treasured £30 - all I had left! "Make sure you're out before 6am," I was told. I was then handed the key with an extremely large key fob; "No way of losing this," I thought. The room was small and just had a single bed and a TV, but at least I was out of the cold.

I then texted my boss, telling him that I had been kicked out of the room I was renting and was now in digs on Margate seafront. I called Laura in London. She told me as soon as she had some money she would try and come down to see me. When I got off the phone my boss had texted back to say he would be round at 5:30am. Now to try and get cleaned up and ready for bed. I had a nice clean towel that was hanging over the radiator. So I used the shared bathroom and was soon in bed.

When I woke up I decided it would be a good idea to get my body temperature up by having another hot shower, but this time I had to queue to use the bathroom. By the time my turn came the floor was soaked and the toilet had obviously seen a lot of action, the smell was unbelievable.

I came downstairs and tried to find the owner to hand back the key. They must have started breakfast very early because all I could smell was bacon and sausages. My belly started to grumble at the thought of such luxuries!

I left having not eaten for nearly 24 hours. A restless night's sleep and no food wasn't the best way to start the day.

I jumped into my boss's work van which was waiting outside. I told him about what had happened; he pulled out his wallet and handed me £70. It wasn't much to him, but to me, it was a huge lifeline.

Matt was a very tall and well-built Cockney; he sounded like he should be in a Danny Dyer movie as one of the main characters. Although he used to work me very hard, I always feel he got the very best out of me. He had obviously grown up in a tough environment when working and was just passing on how he was taught to everyone else. I had already learned a lot about discipline and determination from him.

On the way to work we spoke about what my next steps were. He had a friend who had a few places across Thanet to rent, so gave him a ring. The only thing he had available was a cheap flat in Cliftonville. I wasn't in a position to be picky, and immediately snapped it up. I was told it needed a full renovation and wasn't ready to be lived in, but I just needed a place to stay while I got my life in order. So we both agreed to it on a temporary basis.

After work, Matt drove me to his nan's house. She was living in a nursing home and Matt had asked her if it was okay to lend me some things for the flat, as it was completely unfurnished. I didn't feel very comfortable with this as I've always had a great sense of respect for the elderly, and it felt a bit like I was taking advantage of her.

I had little choice though, so despite my reservations I just had to swallow my pride and take everything I needed. This amounted to a mattress, a deep fat fryer, microwave, some bed sheets and blankets, a portable alarm clock and a pillow.

After packing up the van we then drove around to what would be my new home. As we drove up the road in Cliftonville where my new flat was situated I looked out of the window. I saw that many of the streetlights were broken, sofas and fridge freezers had been dumped on the footpaths, people were hanging around smoking, with hoodies up hiding their faces, and big bottles of white lightning for their dinner.

We pulled up outside the building and I opened the van door. The cold wind instantly hit me in my face – it was winter and the nights closed in fast.

I looked up and could see Matt's friend was standing by the front door, and I was introduced to him. He told me that he was having problems with the electric meter as the previous tenants had done something dodgy with it. We walked into the hall and he tried the light, but it didn't work. He got a torch out of his pocket and told me to follow him up the stairs. The stairs weren't carpeted and every step sounded with a thud then a creak. Finally, we reached the fourth floor which was right at the top. The landlord opened the door and it led straight into the kitchen. I turned the light on and could see it was completely bare, no doors on any of the cupboards, and the only other thing that was left was the sink. I walked around to my left into what was the front room, I tried the light but it didn't have a bulb. I then walked around the whole flat and found I had just one light bulb for all the rooms, so I couldn't really see anything.

Matt brought some of my new things up. As I gave him a hand I tried to be very enthusiastic about the flat, trying not to be ungrateful. After they left and I was on my own, I took the bulb from the kitchen and put it in each of the rooms so I could have a look around. The whole flat had nothing but creaky floorboards, the windows didn't have any curtains and everyone from across the street could see in. The bathroom had one of those very old baths that was in need of a bloody good clean, as were the toilet and sink. The bedroom had huge bulges in the walls which were covered in black mould. The stench of dampness hit the back of my throat. I quickly closed the door and decided to use the front room as my bedroom.

I was still filthy from work and had to have some sort of a wash, so I turned on the hot tap aware I had only just turned the boiler on, just wishing hot water would pour out, but no. Not even a steady stream of water came from the hot tap. It made a load of noise and spurted a few times, then delivered just a dribble of cold water. I turned the cold tap on which worked fine. I washed the worst of the dirt and cobwebs from the bottom of the bath and got undressed. I got in the bath and knelt down, then started washing myself with the cold water in what felt like the Antarctic. I got out and put on the only clean clothes I had, trying to get any sort of warmth to my frozen skin.

Matt had given me a mattress and it was leaning up against the kitchen wall, so I pulled that in and laid it on the floor of the front room. I had a few blankets and put them over it. I laid down on the mattress and could feel a strong breeze coming from the window, so I covered that with a sheet, which served a double purpose - stopping the breeze whilst also stopping my new neighbours from peering in.

I turned the light off and climbed back into bed. It was absolutely freezing and I could see my breath. I looked over to the window to find that the only streetlight that wasn't broken was shining right in. The sheet I put up over the window was literally billowing as the bitter wind blew through the closed window. It looked like the sail from a yacht.

Unable to sleep, my mind went into overdrive and I began to feel incredibly lonely. I tried calling Laura but didn't have any credit. We used to save a few pence of credit when we didn't have any money, just enough to prank call each other when we wanted to talk. I'd hoped that she'd see the missed call and ring back. After a few times I gave up, feeling like I had no one in the world. Then it just became all too much and I started crying my eyes out. I must have cried myself to sleep.

However, the sleep didn't last long because a piercing scream put an end to that. I went to the window and could see a group of people shouting at each other in a language that I didn't recognise. Then a fight broke out, and I watched a woman run from her house. I thought she was going to break it up but then she joined in! I jumped back into bed and pulled the blanket over my head, at least this was a bit warmer. Giving up on getting any further sleep I cast my mind back to my time in Royal Marines training.

In my training, they had instilled the mindset of NEVER GIVE UP. I remember a corporal once telling me, "You can curl up in some corner and die, or you can get back up and start again. Remember this saying: 'I will succeed. Always, will I take another step. If that is to no avail, I will take another and yet another. In truth, one step at a time is not too difficult. I will persist until I succeed.'"

Before I joined the Royal Marines I was headed down a very dark path. I was fighting every weekend and getting in constant trouble with the police. I was so lucky I didn't end up with a criminal record.

I was out one night and was dancing in a nightclub, this was before I met Laura. I saw a girl that caught my eye so I decided to dance towards her. It was something reminiscent of a dance from 'The Inbetweeners'. Then before I got anywhere near her one of her friends tapped me on the shoulder, leaned in and said, "Watch out, her other half is in the Royal Marines."

That was it, I just stood there, looking at the ceiling. *Royal Marines*. I knew they had a reputation for being tough. I wanted that, I wanted people to say 'watch out' for *me*. After that I began my application to join, and alongside working for Matt I started running in the evenings. I ran three to five miles every day. Even running and training this much didn't prepare me for the incredibly difficult training the Royal Marines is renowned for.

The Royal Marines training is the hardest professional infantry training in the world. It's 32 weeks, getting harder and harder as it goes on. The first few weeks are mostly admin, ironing your shirts and folding your kit ready for inspections. During training you are nicknamed a 'Nod', this is because you are worked to the bone all day and live off around three hours sleep every night, so you are nodding off every time you sit down. The standard punishment was fifty push-ups.

The corporal would come in to make sure you were awake at a certain time. If one person was still in bed, all the recruits had to do fifty push-ups. Late out of the showers? Fifty push-ups. Late back from breakfast? Fifty push-ups. Late for drill? Fifty push-ups. This went on through the day and night. I reckon we probably did around five hundred a day.

The year I joined was in 2009, and most of the trainers had already completed tours of duty in Afghanistan and Iraq. They were making sure we were fully trained to go because their best mates would soon be relying on us to watch their backs.

That's what it was like in there, it's friendship like no other, not like on civvy street. Your friends are your best friends, you watch out for each other and make sure you never forget anyone and no one is left behind. I hadn't experienced friends like this before. Before I joined up I didn't really have any friends in civvy street.

I remember on one particular run I felt so much pride for my friends because they wouldn't let me go. We had been running for miles and getting close to the end. I was desperately trying to finish as we were running as a squad in step. I began to slow down, I was running in the middle of three columns, so I had someone to my left and right. I was trying to gulp in as much air as I could, but my legs started to slow. They started whispering, "Come on Brett, stay with us… Come on mate!" I pushed on and managed to keep in step, but with the finish line in sight I started slowing again. I felt my shorts tighten as two fists grabbed each side. They had both taken a hold of my shorts saying, "You're not going anywhere mate."

I was always desperate to help everyone out after that. I loved the feeling that gave me. So when I saw someone struggling with kit or sewing, I would give them a hand.

On one exercise in training we were on Dartmoor, with full

bergan (army slang for backpack) packed with kit and equipment, then webbing around your waist with ammunition and grenades, then your rifle. The uniform consisted of a helmet and camouflage clothing.

We were yomping (walking) back on a night navigation; it was the early hours and the fog had just come in so close you couldn't even see your hand in front of your face. We were in a section of about five or six. We tried to take a shortcut back and jumped a fence, but as we were walking I felt the whole ground beneath our feet move, it was like walking on a waterbed.

"Did anyone else feel that?" I said. "Nah Brett, not enough sleep mate, you're imagining it again." Just as he finished speaking our map reader fell through the ground up to his chest in water. I hadn't imagined it, we had just walked straight into a bog, and my god did it stink. We had to drag the poor guy out and yomp the longest way around to get back to camp.

After a couple of hours sleep the daylight started creeping in and the training team came to wake us up, asking, "Anyone seen 3 section?!"

In that section were the two guys who had helped me on the run. We all said, "No, Corporal." He then said, "They're lost and we don't have any comms with them. We need some volunteers to come help us find them. It'll mean yomping some more. Anyone who is in, come see us at the Land Rover."

These were my mates. Well, they all were, but these were the ones who didn't let me fall behind on that run. I looked down at my feet, they were wrecked. I had lost several toenails from the miles and miles of yomping over the past few days and nights, they were blistered and bleeding and one of my bootlaces had snapped on the yomp the night before.

When I'd got back, I had talcum-powdered my feet before getting a couple of hours' sleep in my sleeping bag. I just had to not think about the pain. I got some surgical tape from my bag and

The Dark and Lonely Road

wrapped it around each of my toes and all over my feet; I tied a knot in the snapped lace, put some dry socks on, put on my webbing and grabbed my rifle; I limped down to the Land Rover.

I was the first one there. "Brett, you sure you're good to go, you look like you're limping a bit there?" "Yes corporal, but those are my mates up there and who knows what condition they're in, one of them might be injured. We don't leave anyone behind."

I didn't end up yomping very far in the end because the training team kept me in the Land Rover with some binoculars looking out the window. We found our mates once the fog completely disappeared, then we all came back to camp to celebrate the Royal Marines' birthday with a shot of rum.

Some of the lads in training pushed their bodies so hard they would often break, quite literally. One recruit on that exercise broke his ankle and still kept going, another left the tape on his feet too long, then when he eventually took it off most of the skin came off with it.

Everyone pushed their bodies so hard that by the end of the 32 weeks training when you complete thirty miles across Dartmoor in eight hours and receive the greatest prize of all, the Green Beret, you have the fitness levels of a professional athlete.

Just to put that into context. When I joined you had to do two mile-and-a-half runs. The first mile-and-a-half is a squad run to be done in twelve minutes. Then you have a one-minute break and it's a "best effort" for the next mile-and-a-half, but it has to be under ten minutes.

My first attempt at the second mile-and-a-half was 9:55. I was five seconds shy of failing. Halfway through training you do this again, but in high-leg combat boots. My time for the second mile and a half was down to 8:20. That's how much fitness you get, that's how much you are trained.

During the Falklands War the Argentinians ruled out a British attack because they said no one could walk fifty-six miles in three

The Dreamer

days. But the Brits did. Carrying 36kg of equipment they yomped fifty-six miles in three days then fought the Argentinians. During World War 2, the commando unit was formed by Winston Churchill, and they became such a nuisance to the Nazis that Adolf Hitler ordered any Commandos to be shot, rather than be treated like prisoners of war.

Ultimately, I didn't complete my Royal Marines training. I'd been seeing Laura for three years before joining, and for the last six months of that time we were both unemployed. I was living with my parents. They had quite old-fashioned values and wouldn't let Laura stay over. We didn't have a lot of money, so a romantic weekend in a hotel was out of the question. So, we'd fill our rucksacks with supplies and a small tent and disappear into the woods for a few days. We'd take Laura's dog. We found a favourite spot and would return to it time after time. Many, many lovely days and nights were spent in those woods. We had absolutely nothing and no jobs - we just had each other and were so very happy to just be together. But now I was in the Marines I wasn't coming home much, and she moved to London. It's a very long time to be away from someone. At the beginning we would be writing and phoning all the time, then near the end of my training I would be calling her but getting no answer, and letters stopped coming.

Then one day I phoned and she answered. As we were talking she seemed distant and I could hear a man's voice in the background. I asked who it was. At first she denied there was anyone there, but as I persisted, she then told me it was 'just a friend'. I put down the phone and felt like I was trapped. When you're on a military base, the barbed wire they put up around the base to keep people out can sometimes feel like a prison keeping you in. As the weeks went by, Laura's 'friend' began spending more and more time with her. I began to mess up in my daily training and all I wanted was to leave and come back to Laura before I lost her. She was all I had and all I ever knew.

The Dark and Lonely Road

I had to ask my commanding officer for permission to leave the Royal Marines training after telling him my head just wasn't in it anymore. I felt like a danger to my mates, I felt like their training was being impeded because I was now the weak link. He reluctantly agreed and told me I could rejoin anytime.

That probably has to be the biggest regret of my life. The Royal Marines Commando training centre has its own platform for the local train. When I boarded the train and could see other recruits training on the assault course it felt like I was leaving home. All my friends would soon be going to Afghanistan and I wouldn't be there to watch out for them.

I went back home to live with my parents again. Laura insisted nothing had happened and we kind of patched things up. But she was still living in London and I had to go back to Thanet as it was the only place I could find work.

I then followed my RM mates on social media as a few weeks later they all passed their Royal Marines Commando tests – nine-mile speed march carrying full fighting order in ninety minutes; the endurance course consisting of two miles of running across moorland and crawling through tunnels; then a four-mile run back to camp followed by a marksman test; the Tarzan assault course. And then the final test, the thirty-miler - thirty miles across Dartmoor with full fighting kit in eight hours. When you complete the thirty-miler you are then presented with your Green Beret.

It's more than just a beret, it's a rite of passage, a badge of honour.

You only touch the green beret when you earn it. I still have not touched one to this day and will never do so. The Royal Marines will always have a place in my heart. The months I was in there felt like an eternity and it changed my life for the better. That fear of giving up on something has stuck with me, so whenever I feel like giving up, I think back to that feeling of leaving the Royal Marines. I never want to feel beaten like that again.

The Dreamer

I looked around the room in the flat and thought to myself, "Remember this place because one day you will remember how far you have come." I didn't really know how far I was going to go or where I was going, but I couldn't continue running my life like I had up to then.

Eureka

Over the next few days I began to settle in. I was always good at finding bargains and would make sure I would go down to Tesco at a certain time of day so I could get the reduced-price food that they put out. I had a small deep fat fryer and would cook cheap sausages and chips in it. I also had a kettle. I don't drink hot drinks but it was great for 10p noodles. Bread was a bit of a godsend, it was around 50p a loaf, and I lived on chip butties and sausage sandwiches. It was filling enough for me to have a good meal and the calories I needed for work, yet spending very little money.

I'd also bought a halogen space heater. It was my tiny piece of heaven. I could only afford for it to be on when I was absolutely freezing, so I would wait until the cold became unbearable before using it. I washed my clothes in the bath with Poundland washing-up liquid, and hung them on makeshift hangers. They rarely properly dried, and I often had to go to work wearing damp clothes. When temperatures were struggling to get above minus it wasn't ideal. I often would go to work in soaked tracksuit bottoms, hoping I could stay in the lorry long enough for them to dry. I probably smelt musty as hell, as musty as my mood, but Matt knew I was struggling. Despite being strict in a lot of ways, he believed he knew which battles were worth fighting.

One day, back in the summer, we'd been hand-laying boiling hot tarmac. You have to do it fast. I knew I didn't even have a second to do up my laces, but it was midday and I was so hot I felt like I was going to pass out. So I walked over to the van to get a drink. He came running over asking what I was doing. When I said I wanted a drink he replied, "We all want a drink Dave! Come on back to work!!" Then he began pulling me back to the job.

That was Matt's work ethic. While driving to the job he was

The Dreamer

constantly on the phone, hands-free, arranging as much work as he could lay his hands on. Then, when he wasn't driving and someone else was, he would eat as much of his lunch and drink as much as he could to get through the day without stopping. Stopping meant the performance dropped; if performance dropped, he would lose his company's brilliant reputation for always delivering results. I guess the time I tried to get a sip of water when I should have been working made him think it would affect the job and we might not be able to finish it. So on that occasion, I had to wait for a drink until the drive home.

When I was doing sewer work, being the smallest on site, I was always 'volunteered' to go down the manholes to fix them. 'Volunteered' was always, "Dave, you're perfect for this, I'm too big to go down there." One of these 'volunteered' moments was when we had to retrieve a manhole cover that had come loose and dropped down a shaft after a car had driven over it.

For this to take place, a tripod with a winch attached was set up above the open manhole. The cable from the winch was reeled out and came through the top of the tripod so the cable would run directly down the chamber of the manhole. I had a waterproof onesie with Wellington boots attached, and I duct-taped my gloves around my wrists to stop anything getting in.

I then had to don my harness and get hooked on the cable. Once hooked on, I sat down on the edge of the manhole with my legs dangling, waiting for the winchman to take my weight.

Once I felt the snag of my harness and was reassured it could take my weight, I gently eased into the manhole chamber, swaying gently, with half my body in the chamber and half still poking out of the manhole. Then I was slowly lowered. It was around twelve meters down. Most people don't think twice about walking over a manhole cover, but some of these chambers are deep... And I mean deep. I would think twice about walking over a broken manhole cover, it could send you into hell.

The gas detector I had attached around my waist would beep every few seconds, constantly scanning the air to make sure it wasn't toxic and had enough oxygen. This loud beep was a constant reminder of how dangerous the job really is. If I looked up, I could see the open manhole becoming ever more distant. The smell in the air was old and musky, a bit like the smell in a deep dark cave. As I got closer to the bottom, I could hear the roar of the torrent of sewage beneath my feet becoming more potent.

I'd reached the point where I could no longer feel my feet dragging on the side of the slimy brick chamber. The winch then lowered me into a space about the same size as a small hotel bathroom. The open pipe on either side was around one metre tall.

I was lowered down inch by inch into the raging torrent of sewage. First my feet, then my knees and slowly up to my waist until I felt the bottom of the sewer pipe and could stand. I shouted up to the winchman telling him to stop. The sewage smashed into my legs making it hard to even stand, the bottom of the pipe was really slippery, worsening my grip.

The chamber where the pipe entered, and where I was now standing, became wider and the torrent pushed me closer to the pipeline heading out of the chamber. Now I was under a ledge and couldn't see my way out. I looked up and could see the cable rubbing the brickwork of the narrow chimney heading upwards. The cable was tight on my harness, it was the only thing keeping me standing upright, it was my lifeline. The steam from the sewage condensed on the top of the concrete ledge I was standing under and dripped all over me.

In this hellhole I had to try and feel with my boots for the fallen cover. I now had to fight hard to keep one foot planted on the bottom of the slippery wet sewage line and fight to push my other foot forward, so I would be back under the chamber leading out, while also trying to feel around for the lid to the manhole cover.

After managing to find it, I then had to try to move it with my boots into a position where I could try to grab it. The flow from the sewage was around my waist and I managed to get the lid of the cover between my legs. I shouted up for a hook to be sent down via rope. The hook is attached to a wooden pole, and I grabbed it as it came down.

Now I was trying to hold both the cover and the hook in my hands. Bad idea. The hook slipped out and disappeared into the darkness. I turned and shone my torch down the sewer line. I couldn't see anything, the steam from the sewage stopped the light, a bit like trying to put on full beams in the fog.

Looking down the line into the darkness I started to think about what would happen if this cable somehow became loose from my harness and I would follow the same route as the hook. The cable behind me was all twisted by now; imagine if it suddenly unlocked and I was unhooked. That sewage flow would probably carry me for miles and if I somehow survived being dragged down the endless sewage network, I'd come to a point where my body wouldn't fit and... Well, I'll let you imagine the rest. There must be easier ways to earn a living.

Anyway, I considered my options. We could send a rope down and tie it to the cover. Then I could come up first, and then try to pull it up. But what if it came loose and fell back down? I only wanted to do this once, this thing was coming with me. Only one way out now, I would have to grip the manhole cover in my arms and the winchman would have to pull me up.

At around 25kg and as slippery as butter, this was going to prove quite a challenge. The winch started to slowly pull me back out, one inch at a time. I was getting closer to that circle of blue sky above, which at that moment looked like heaven. Then halfway up the winch stopped. I shouted up, "What's going on!" The winchman said, "The winch is making funny noises, it might be too heavy, I'm just checking it." So there I was, dangling over hell, my life in his hands. If I were to drop the cover and say, "Fuck it, get me out of here!" I would definitely lose my job or be told, "We don't have any work for you anymore." Being self-employed, companies can call you into work one week, then if they don't like you, you are told, "No work this week."

I couldn't afford to be out of work. I just had to hold onto this cover. I could feel my arms burning, I shouted up again urging the winchman to hurry up.

The slow rise to the top started again. Once my head came out of the chamber I took the biggest gulp of fresh air and launched the cover over to the side. You'd think the wages would be pretty good for this? I was on a wage that I could just about live on, only to go back to a house that was destroying my soul further.

I couldn't carry on like this. I decided to make a change in my life. I was going to get my own house and have an income that didn't require me to work in such dangerous places.

So how was I going to get out of my current situation? I looked in newspapers and asked around at offices near where we worked to see if there were any jobs going. I wanted to work in an office, you're nice and safe in there. But I didn't have the qualifications that lots of jobs asked for. I couldn't even spell, and I didn't have many office skills. At least I didn't think I did. But one day I got it into my head that rather than working for someone else, maybe I could start my own business. Doing what - I had no clue, but once I'd had the thought, there was no getting rid of it.

I would sleep with a pen and paper next to my mattress, just in case I thought up a great idea in the middle of the night, and I could then write it down before I forgot it. I became obsessed with trying to find solutions to problems. I'd always thought that it was a strength of mine, and one that I enjoyed. I started thinking small. Maybe I could start a sewage company in my area? Then I decided to think bigger. I began thinking about problems in the world, rubbish left on the side of motorways, how can I make a device that would pick it up? Charging phones on the go was also a big problem. I thought the busy people of London would definitely need something like a portable battery pack if their phone was running low while they were on the move. Something where you could pick it up, charge your phone and drop it off when you are done. But every time I thought of an idea I would go through it in my head and realise you would need a lot of money to start something like that. I needed to find something that would cost relatively little to start but could grow.

I could lose hours at a time, the day passing by, just fantasising about the things I could do. Each time I had a brilliant idea, that was it... I had it... I thought I had solved it, figured it all out. I had an idea for a wheelbarrow - rather than using a thin wheel you could use a bigger wheel. Like the size of a football; this would make it easier to push through tough muddy fields. But James Dyson had already thought of that. He had first put it on a wheelbarrow, then later he put the huge ball on one of his vacuum cleaners.

I spent a lot of time daydreaming about what would happen when I finally found my big idea, when I was finally in charge, telling other people what to do. I'd be a kind boss, I decided. And fair. Maybe through my work I'd even be able to make a positive change to peoples' lives – people like me!

I would get so excited, planning what I would need to do, my thoughts running away with themselves. But then I would do some research and find out that it had already been done, or already existed, and I would come crashing back down to Earth. It was very frustrating. It was also exhausting, but I was determined. I told my workmates I was trying to find a new idea or invention to try and better myself, and I often shared some ideas with them.

They found the whole thing hilarious. They thought I had my head in the clouds.

"You may as well go and buy a lottery ticket. Same odds," one mate told me.

They all nodded their heads in agreement.

"There aren't any new ideas. Everything decent has already been thought up," said another.

This hit a nerve, as it was exactly what I had been finding – that every time I thought of a business, a similar one existed.

"How can all the ideas have gone?" I asked him. "People invent new things and new businesses every day."

"Alright then. Suppose you come up with something good. What do you do then?"

It was a fair point. I didn't know the answer. But I wasn't going to let that stop me.

Then one day it happened. It was a rare moment. I was sitting in the van waiting for a delivery of tarmac, listening to the news on the radio. The announcer reported that Connexions Centres, a government initiative to get young people back to work, was closing down. This was greeted with criticism as there were over a million 16-25's out of work. 'The lost generation' was how the reporter described them.

That was it. My mind then went into overdrive. How can I help these young people get back to work and make a business out of it? I grabbed an old piece of paper and started to make notes, a kind of brainstorming like I remembered doing at school.

I wrote the problem in the middle of the page – 'Young people lose government support in getting work. They need a new way to find jobs.' Then I drew lines coming out of the problem across the page. I would then write down the things that I could do to help, and what my business would do. Giving advice was my first thought, I could give advice, then try to inspire people with inspirational stories. It's hard being out of work, morale is low. I wanted to create a website that would lift a jobseeker's morale and make it a place they would enjoy visiting, something that said, "Don't give up, you can do this!" Then there's the practical stuff. I could help them with filling in application forms, with creating a CV, pointing people in the direction of good and cheap training courses.

The Dreamer

But the business would also need to make money. Would I have to sell advertising to companies, or maybe jobs could be displayed on a website for a fee? Did I even have the skills and know-how to do all this? I remember when I was at school and sitting in an IT class, we all had to create a website. The teacher talked us through it, and from what I could remember it wasn't too hard. Maybe I could find someone to do it for me? Surely it wouldn't cost too much for a simple website. If my boss could make a website for his business, I was sure I could find a way, even if it meant more hours working in the sewers of hell, it was all for the greater good.

I started scribbling down all my ideas and when I'd finished, it all started to come together and I could see it would work. It was going to be the UK's first job search website devoted to helping 16-25's get back to work, listing only entry-level jobs. All jobs would need a maximum of two years' experience. All the job-seeker would have to do is type in their location and a list would be shown of suitable vacancies in their area that they would have a decent chance of getting. I hadn't felt so excited for longer than I could remember.

Maybe this was the great idea that was going to get me my dream job, and my dream house.

After work, I went straight to an internet café in Cliftonville. I walked in and paid a pound for one hour's internet. I apprehensively searched for anything similar online. To my delight, and relief, I couldn't really find anything. Having some time left, I looked into the legal implications of limiting applications to a certain age range. I found that I couldn't stop people from applying for jobs based on their age, so I decided on a 'targeting 16-25's' slogan. This just meant my business would be built to suit this age range, I wouldn't stop anyone of any age from applying. I then splashed out on another hour's internet time. It meant 10p noodles for dinner, but I was on a roll.

It just seemed to flow and I was coming up with ideas left, right and centre. This was going to be the in place for young people to come and search for jobs. I was going to do it right, I was going to have everything perfect. I put it all into a Word document and printed it out. So protective I was of my idea, my baby, I was even shielding it from the guy behind the counter in case he stole it. Okay, not likely, but I didn't want to take any chances. The next person who saw this document needed to be the person who was going to help me make it work!

When I returned to my computer, I could see I still had a half hour left, so I picked up the earphones and started listening to some music, my head bopping away, with a big smile on my face. I always think it's funny - when you're happy you just listen to the music, when you're sad you listen to the words. I looked up houses, looking for my dream home. Would I stay in the area or would I move away? I began looking at small houses, something realistic to aim for, but then I decided I would aim for a huge, beautiful home. I remember hearing someone say once, "Aim for the stars, and even if you only reach the sky, you're still higher than you were before you started." I then looked at exotic holidays abroad - Las Vegas, Maldives, Bora Bora. How wonderful would it be to be able to afford such luxury? Imagine if I made it that big. Big enough that I could fly around the world exploring new places. Big enough that when I came back home I had my own house waiting for me, somewhere I could call home.

Still with ten minutes left, I started looking for business events. I wanted to be one of the suits that walked around in London, looking all important and successful, someone who has made it in life. I stumbled across an event in London Olympia that was coming up within the next few weeks. A business start-up exhibition. It was fate, surely. Or maybe gut instinct. Whatever it was, I knew that I had to go and show off my new idea. I had no idea who I was showing it off to, but I just wanted to talk to people about how to get started.

I booked a ticket for the event. I could have just wasted the very little money that I had for absolutely nothing, or I could have just made the best investment of my life. I didn't know which of the two it was yet, but I was optimistic and high on adrenaline, completely buzzed by the thought of making my idea into a real business. I found a bed-and-breakfast in London where I could stay over, as it was a two-day event. Luckily it was a 'book now, pay when you arrive' deal so I just had to scrimp the money together over the next few weeks.

I printed my ticket for Olympia and also a picture of my dream house. It was a million-pound house with a swimming pool and a Lamborghini on the driveway. "Aim for the stars!"

This was to become my star that I would aim for. As I walked out of the internet café, heading back to the flat, I felt lost in excitement. I was full of dreams. I was going to be just like those businessmen you see in London. All suited and booted. Walking around looking important with a briefcase and the latest iPhone, making calls, sending emails, running a business. No more wet clothes to work, no more hi-vis bomber jackets, I was going to make it.

I went to work the next day and told everyone I had my big new idea… and they all pretty much laughed in my face. They told me that it was never going to work, not to even bother, someone with more money than me would have thought of that already, that's the reason why it hasn't been done, because someone with a real education has probably tried it and failed.

"What chance are you going to have? You work in the sewers!"

Their response made me start to doubt myself and my idea, but I couldn't stop thinking of this event in London. Two days of my life. See what businesspeople think of my idea. If those people who are a success in expensive new suits say yes, then I know it will work. Just keep believing. When a boxer believes they can win a fight, it definitely helps. When they are constantly doubting themselves, I'm sure they wouldn't make it past the first round.

London's Calling

As the days then started to lead up to the event, I asked one of my friends to go to my parents and try and get some of my clothes. I couldn't do it myself because I'd quickly fallen out with my parents after moving back there once I'd left the Marines.

The different debt collectors who kept coming round to the house weekly were what caused our relationship to break down. I can't even remember what they were for, I had so many. My parents had got fed up and wanted me out, so I just left. I was ashamed I'd got myself into such a terrible situation. My career wasn't anything to be proud of and I had debts coming out of my ears. Neighbours would see bailiffs knocking on the door constantly. My parents had worked hard to get a nice house and had two cars on the drive... but me for a son. In my eyes, it wasn't much to be proud of.

I went from friend's house to friend's house outstaying my welcome on each occasion, until I just had to try and pay for a spare room in someone's house and ended up in my dismal flat. Laura was miles away and I was all alone. So this was something I had to do alone. No one else knew about my plan, and I didn't want anyone to spoil it. Sometimes all that people have in this world is hope and you should never take that away from them, I wasn't about to lose mine by telling someone. I texted Laura to say I would be coming to London, but didn't get a reply.

When I eventually got hold of some of my clothes, I looked through them and found some bits I could wear to the event. I had some trousers and a shirt, and I found some old shoes in there as well. I wanted to make sure I looked the absolute best I could, I'm representing my idea, after all. So I needed to make sure I looked perfect, so it would look like I had the perfect idea.

I went down to Primark and found a nice cheap tie. I looked at the blazers but they were way out of my price range. I had a black coat at home which would have to do. One thing the Royal Marines training teaches you is how to iron your clothes and how to make yourself presentable, and I'd have the coat spick and span in no time. I also wanted something to carry all of my paperwork in, so I searched for briefcases. I found them either old-fashioned or too expensive. Instead, I went for a laptop bag. It was nice and cheap, and maybe people would think that I had a laptop in there too!

The night before the event came, I was so nervous. By this time I had bought a TV/video player and bought some video tapes from a charity shop for ten pence each. I didn't have any TV channels so I just had to settle for movies. I played them in the background to keep me company, it's amazing how much someone else's voice in the background can keep you company. I was just sitting there thinking over everything in my head; sometimes I would just lay under my blankets, imagining how it was all going to pan out.

I got all my clothes ready and hung them on a clothes hook on the wall, then I noticed that I had a hole in the bottom of my shoe. It was right underneath my middle toe. I got some old cardboard I had lying about and stuffed it inside. Job done. I then noticed further bad news as I stood up looking at my clothes. My trousers had a rip in the crotch area. I walked around the flat to try and find something I could use to fix it, and all I could find was a Red Nose Day badge. It would have to do. I put it on the inside of my trousers to act as a makeshift safety pin. I then got a black felt-tip pen and tried to darken the metal so it wasn't so shiny. Hopefully no one would see it and hopefully it would stay in place! I could imagine that being painful if it came undone when I went to sit down!

While I was lying in bed I heard a lot of shouting again from outside, accompanied by some loud bangs. I looked out of the window and saw a group of people who were either very drunk or high on something, or both. They were walking down the street screaming and kicking mirrors off the parked cars. All the car alarms were going off and then they started jumping on top of the cars. Neighbours ran out and it all started kicking off again. I quickly got back into bed, more determined than ever that I had to get out of this place.

I woke up in the morning and started to prepare myself for the next two big days. I had been down to the internet café and designed some leaflets. I had also ordered some very cheap business cards from VistaPrint. I had also by this time designed my company logo. My recruitment website was going to be the next best thing.

I put all my things in my new laptop bag (still without a laptop!) and walked to Margate train station. Once on the train I sat down and heard over the speaker, "London Victoria." That was my stop, I was off to London. Sitting on the train and off to London for 'business'. I was so excited. I looked around the train and could see some other people in suits, and I felt like I was one of them. I put my earphones in and started listening to my music. I find music can be very powerful.

It helps me unwind one moment, get fired up the next. Used correctly it can be a huge motivational tool. I definitely feel there is a human connection between music and state of mind, if you think about it. You want to listen to slow music when you are down, maybe to get the tears out. But when you hit the gym it's fast pumping music to keep your heart racing. Well, it is for me anyway.

I got off at London Victoria and walked around the station trying to find the underground, not knowing where to go. I hadn't been to London on the train on my own before; if I ever came to London I would meet Laura at the station and she would show me where to go. The station was completely packed, people rushing about in all directions, showing little regard for anyone. I finally found the way to the underground. The London Underground is a complete maze if you haven't been on it before, what with the coloured lines and the fast pace everyone sets as they head towards the platforms or the exit. I was beginning to realise why they called it the rat race! After a

The Dreamer

while of bumbling around the underground, I finally made it onto the right train to Olympia. Music still playing in my ears and my heart starting to beat increasingly faster. What would this place be like? What sort of things will there be?

I finally arrived at the platform for Olympia and could see the building, it was huge!

Even though I was early, there was already a long queue and I was soon standing at the end of it. I looked at the other people who were attending. They nearly all seemed to be wearing expensive suits, nice shiny watches, and perfectly polished shoes. They all spoke with an educated voice, not like me, a common boy from the streets of Margate. Not for the first time I started to doubt myself, looking down to the ground as I walked. I felt like these people were better than me and I was a fake. It didn't feel like I belonged there. I stood there looking at my clothes and down towards my dull shoes, still feeling the cardboard stopping my toes from popping out the bottom. The waiting was the worst thing, and I started to feel that all I wanted to do was to go home. Did I seriously think something would come of this? Did I even stand a chance? What did I have to offer other than just one idea thought up on the back of a scrap piece of paper?

Then I thought that I had paid all this money for the event when I didn't have a lot, and realised that I had to go through with it. I had to stay. I owed it to myself to give it a shot. Otherwise, all my planning and preparation would have been for nothing. I at least had to try. Sometimes in life regret isn't about the things we did do, it's about the things we didn't do.

I was starting to be in my own little bubble, music still blasting in my ears. The world is locked out, all the people here can't talk to me, not as long as I am in my protective bubble.

The doors opened and in I walked. It was as if someone had opened a shopping centre and everything was half price. Everyone rushed in through the doors and everything started to become very overwhelming.

There were stands everywhere. Everything was organised into rows and sections, with fancy expensive banners and posters everywhere. Then immediately I was hit with people shoving leaflets in my face. Big smiles all over their faces, coming up and trying to talk to me about business opportunities. "Would you like this service? What about this?"

I started to dodge them, moving around each stall, but they wouldn't give up. I must have been approached by every single salesperson. I was beginning to think that I had 'easy target' tattooed on my forehead. Within minutes I had business cards in one hand, leaflets in the other. I'd even been given a carrier bag with something in it at some point. Where it all came from is still a bit of a blur. It was all too much. I felt overwhelmed. I had no idea what I was meant to be doing or saying. My heart was racing. I looked around and saw a coffee shop at the far end and I just started walking towards it. Once in there I let out a sigh of relief and tried to get myself ready for going back out and trying again. I looked at the things I had in my hand and threw some of the stuff away that I didn't need but kept some of the others as I thought they may come in handy in the future. I thought about using the designs or some of the ideas, trying to utilise anything I could to gain some sort of advantage. Sometimes it's okay to stand on the shoulders of geniuses, it means you can copy what they do and see a bit further ahead.

I then decided to grab a drink. I thought Tesco at full price was expensive, but this was a whole new ball game. I counted out my coins and could only afford a bottle of water. I was really hungry but would have needed a mortgage to get a sandwich or a 'panini', never even heard of one of these before. I found a seat tucked away in the corner and sat down. I pulled out my laptop bag and had a look at the map I'd got when I entered. Within it was a programme, and I found a few lectures being given by some very prestigious business people.

The Dreamer

I thought it would be a good idea to go and have a listen to see what they had to say. There were so many questions I already had about starting my business and I had so much to learn. It was costing me almost every penny I had to attend the event so I wanted to make the most of it; and I wasn't going to learn much by sitting in this overpriced coffee shop.

I then got myself up and began darting across the hall, dodging leaflet wielders. I went from one lecture to the next for the rest of the morning. I picked up a lot of interesting business tips, writing them all down. The thing that struck me was that research was key to any business, you should always research everything, making sure you are one step ahead every time.

Networking was something I had never heard of before. But it was a posh word for 'talking to others', not something I was very good at. But some of the best business advertising is through word of mouth. I learned that if you give a good service, people talk. They even gave advice on getting your business into a simple 20-second pitch, making it so simple a child could understand. They weren't being condescending, just pointing out that people are busy. They said your pitch could raise twenty further questions before people truly understand what it is you are doing.

'Smile and dial' was something I had never heard of, but it meant if you smile when you make calls your voice will sound more upbeat. Other tips included being honest about mistakes, because everyone makes them. People appreciate being told the truth, no one likes being lied to. And go for quality, not quantity. Build a business from a solid foundation of happy customers, don't try to run before you can walk. A business is an adventure, not a race. A Richard Branson quote I heard made a particularly big impression on me. "Clients do not come first, employees come first. If you take care of your employees, they will take care of your clients."

I became like a sponge, just trying to absorb as much information as I possibly could.

It was the last lecture of the day I wanted to see, and just like all the others I sat right at the back. I still didn't feel like the other people there. I looked around at what other people were doing. Some were writing things down on a notepad like me, others had iPads and laptops. The lecture was on business confidence, something that interested me because I didn't have any confidence when it came to business. Then the guy presenting it came out and said, "I need a volunteer." That was it, my head went straight down to try and make it look like I was getting something out of my bag. When I looked up a few seconds later I saw that no one had put their hand up. With these sorts of things you just know that if no one volunteers themselves then someone will just be randomly selected. I began to sweat a little at the thought of it. I went straight back down to my bag again, playing with some paperwork, trying my hardest not to look up, saying to myself over and over, "Please God not me, please." Then a young lady stood up and went to the front. Once I heard everyone clapping the lady I stopped faffing about with the paperwork and sat back up, relief flowing through my body.

The guy who was giving the lecture then said, "The hardest part is always stepping up. When people ask for a volunteer, don't be afraid to step forward. Who knows what might happen, you might get something good out of it." He then presented this lady with some expensive business books and some vouchers for VistaPrint. Something I definitely could have done with. As the lecture continued, my head started to rise and I could feel myself getting involved. My confidence had just started to increase. I then began raising my hand and asking questions.

"What's the best way to build confidence for someone who doesn't have any?" I stuttered. "Pride, pride is a good way to start building your confidence," he told me. "Look at you sitting there, you should be proud to be here. Not many people had the courage to come and sit down. But you did. Take pride in whatever you do in life, it could be something so simple as keeping your car clean. The pride you have about keeping a clean car will bring confidence in your ability. Build on this to do other things. A person with pride will flow with confidence."

I sat there and thought, "I need to pride myself in helping others, to help people get back to work. Make sure they have money in the bank and can do things they have always wanted. I can take pride in my business, my business could help so many people get food on the table, I could help them get back to work and pay the rent. Imagine the feeling of helping hundreds of people with their life, this business idea could effectively change the course of a person's whole life for the better."

I had never felt like this before. He explained that everyone has their own battles in life. Everyone has problems. Someone might have more money than other people, but that's not always a good thing. More than anything it's about confidence. If you have no confidence within yourself, you will never achieve what you are trying to do.

That's when I started to look at other people, trying to see why I would be better than this person or that person. Yeah, they may have a fancy laptop, but do they have my motivation? Do they want it as much as me? I walked away feeling a bit more confident in myself.

That's when I started to look at things and people a lot differently. Who knows where that person has got their money from, maybe they had been given it? This is what I asked myself. Maybe they had been spoon-fed their entire life; not knowing how to struggle and get through difficult periods. But I do, I have more strength and power than anyone. I have had to graft for every penny my whole life. Nothing was ever given to me after childhood. As soon as I could earn money I went out and did it, I was just careless when I got it. If I can go down the darkest depths of the sewers to work, or run around all day laying tarmac, or carry kerbs on my shoulders - everything else would be easier compared to that.

I just needed to be guided and get my confidence up.

The lecture then finished. I got up, put my bag over my shoulder, and, as this was the last lecture I wanted to see, I began to head out. But this time I would go straight down the middle to get out. "Let's start building this confidence up!" I told myself.

I think by this time most of the salespeople handing out leaflets had given up for the day and were headed to the coffee shop. I wasn't being approached by many of them anymore.

Just as I was getting to the main door, suddenly I saw a huge stage and a big seating area. It was called 'The Golden Touch'. I could hear a woman introducing someone on stage, she was building up a lot of hype. "Jason has mentored people from around the world to be some of the best entrepreneurs."

'Entrepreneur'... that's a funny word, I thought. I had heard of entrepreneurs before. I stood there thinking to myself. I wonder if I can now call myself one?

"Introducing the UK's best business mentor, I give you Jason Curry!" A very flamboyant man walked onto the stage. Absolutely oozing with confidence as he spoke to everyone. I looked around and could see people were hooked. It was as if this was the person they had been waiting to see all day.

There must have been about 80-100 people sitting in that audience, so many that all the seats had gone and I was standing at the back watching in awe.

Jason started speaking to the audience about how he likes to help people get businesses off the ground and is passionate about mentoring new business owners into creating a big brand.

Jason then turned to his left where there was a big table with three people sitting behind it. These were other investors.

I then quickly began to realise this was something like Dragons' Den. As Jason stopped talking the lady picked up the microphone and introduced two men onto the stage who began introducing themselves and their business.

I looked at each of the investors. "I bet they own their own

The Dreamer

home," I thought to myself. Imagine sitting up there looking at businesses to invest your money into. What a life that must be, no more shovelling tarmac, no more sewers and no more reduced items for dinner!

The two men then began pitching their business to the investors. I can't remember the ideas they were pitching. I don't really think I was listening because I was just entranced by the whole thing.

I wanted to be one of the investors, or at the very least be able to stand up and pitch my idea to them. I thought to myself, "This is where I will do it." I then started to look around the crowd of people watching the event; all those people, watching. I thought to myself, "Could I really stand up in front of all these people and talk about my idea? Let alone in front of those investors who build companies for a living."

The two men pitching their idea were standing with pride behind a lectern with a microphone pointed straight at them. They stood in front of everyone, completely unfazed by the crowd. I started to tune in and listened to the pitch. Their pitch was excellent, they spoke about previous years' revenue, future revenue, profit margins, a growing customer base. Everything they said sounded great. I thought, "These guys are definitely getting some investment."

Once they'd finished, it was the turn of the investors. They started throwing some very intense questions at them, then the questions started getting harder and more thorough. The guys pitching the business were getting absolutely grilled.

"What's your market? How much capital do you have? What are your target earnings for next year again? How much experience do you have?"

I could see they were starting to get very uncomfortable and flummoxed. I started smiling at their predicament, but then suddenly realised I wasn't watching TV anymore. That could be me, and I don't even know what 'capital' is. I imagined me being asked those questions. I didn't understand some of them, let alone know the answers for my business. I hadn't thought about many of those things. How can anyone know these answers? How was I supposed to know how much the business could earn in its first year, before it had even started? And what the hell is a business plan?!

My face dropped as did my confidence. I started to look at myself, looking at my laptopless laptop bag and feeling the cardboard in my shoe. I pulled out the folder I had made for my idea and flicked through it. I had my research at the front of the folder - everything I could find about young people out of work, newspaper clippings, printed sheets from the internet cafe. The Problem. The Solution, my business idea. Pages of dreams, how much money I would charge per job post. My guesstimates on how many jobs I thought I could have on the website per month, how I was going to advertise the jobs. Monthly costs if I were to set up with the GoDaddy website building platform, how much it would cost to secure my domain name, it had to be '.co.uk'. Nothing else was going to cut it.

Revenue guesstimates from Google AdSense: they pay for every click on a banner advertisement shown on your site. It could be anything from £1-£5 per click. I had it written down that I could make a fortune if I could get just the smallest fraction of the one million job seekers on the website. Then that could pave the way for further expansion.

I felt so stupid. What an idiot I was, trying to think I was capable of doing something like that. That's why people always say, "How the other half live," because the other half know the answers to these questions, I thought to myself.

I started walking away, looking for the exit, wondering why I'd been so stupid to spend the little money I had on stuff like this when I had absolutely no chance whatsoever. I felt like my idea was a drop in the ocean, there were so many other people doing what I was trying to do, with such a better chance of achieving it.

I don't have any education, it was never for me. They would be teaching us about how the cells in a leaf work and then let us leave school without knowing anything about taxes, VAT, mortgages, savings, investments, pensions, self-employment, PAYE, interest rates... and the list goes on. You get the point about why I thought it wasn't for me? I wanted *life* education. I was never any good at school because I wasn't interested, and this meant I was classed as 'special needs'.

I was pulled from most of my classes and taken elsewhere for extra 'help'. I never even finished my GCSEs. I started doing construction work at the age of fifteen, pushing wheelbarrows. That was why I now worked on the sewers, because I didn't really have anything going for me. You leave school and banks are throwing money at you left right and centre. Being young and naïve you don't think about the future, then before you know it you end up in a pile of debt. That's why it was so hard to believe that someone like me, someone who shovels other people's shit for a living, could come up with a business that would actually work. What a stupid idea, and I was stupid to pay the money to come here.

I then thought back to all my workmates telling me I was a dreamer and I should just concentrate on trying to rent a better place to live, rather than wasting money on fruitless ideas that won't work.

Laura also kept on at me to forget about my idea and focus on getting a better job, then getting a better place to rent. I now began to think they were all correct. I had just wanted to believe *so much* that it was possible. It felt so good for a while. Depressed, I called Laura and asked her to come and see me, but she said she was busy at work and couldn't leave. What a day this had turned out to be.

I left Olympia and walked back towards the underground, pretty much clueless about where I was headed. I tried my best to work out the underground map and somehow ended up by the Embankment. I walked along the river without any music playing, just trying to gather my thoughts.

I walked under a bridge and saw some homeless people living in a tent. I thought, "It could always be worse." But I had yet to find where I was staying! I wasn't in a rush to get to the B&B, so I just decided to have a little explore around. There was a lovely green park area, so I walked through that and headed up to the busy road.

I looked left and right, not knowing where to go, cars and people just flying around the streets while I'm just stood there. I saw a gentleman in a top hat trying to wave down a black cab. Then he walked out of view. He looked really smart. I wondered what was down the street where he was headed.

I walked along the road and there was an opening between the buildings.

A single road went down to this fabulous hotel, The Savoy. I had definitely heard of this place! The glitz and glamour just scream in your face, everything is sparkling, even the sign 'SAVOY' is lit from behind by a nice green glow.

Green hedges line the road leading to the entrance and a little roundabout had been put in so cars can turn around; on the roundabout there's a water fountain. As you look higher a golden statue of a knight is standing guard over the entrance. Maybe to keep the riff-raff away! They even have their own theatre. How nice would it be just to have a look around inside, let alone be able to stay there for one night. A night in this hotel probably cost as much as two months' wages for me.

It even housed movie stars such as Richard Harris who lived there for years. Looking down the road to the left you could see Gordon Ramsay's restaurant, The Savoy Grill. Imagine eating in Gordon Ramsay's restaurant. I bet the food is out of this world.

Brand new Mercedes came and went, all having their own private chauffeurs, but just as I was looking around I saw a Rolls Royce come past with the Savoy's number plate on!

I just stood completely gobsmacked. "This really is how the other half live!" The man in the top hat that I had seen was now welcoming people into the revolving door to the hotel, but as soon as the Rolls Royce pulled up he immediately opened the rear door and I saw a man and a woman get out, smiling away as they headed into the hotel. I was pretty sure that was Jason, the man I had seen earlier at the Olympia event.

"One day! One day, I'm going to do that! Come on, anyone can do it," I thought, still staring at the hotel.

I took one last look down the little road to the hotel and turned away, making sure that moment was imprinted in my mind, to make me remember why I needed to keep moving forward.

I went to Charing Cross and got on the underground to near where I thought the B&B was. I wandered through the streets, looking for the back-street B&B I had booked online. I finally found it and from the outside it looked okay, it wasn't the Savoy, but hey-ho, beggars can't be choosers. I walked in and got the key to my room and was walking up the stairs when I was hit with a stench of piss - and it wasn't coming from me. I then noticed that someone had urinated up the hallway wall. I got to my room and unlocked the door. It wasn't much, but at least it was warm and had a bed.

I started running the shower and stood there with my hand under the water waiting for the hot water. After waiting and waiting, it became apparent that there wasn't any hot water, so I had to jump in and have a freezing cold shower. I started to feel like I was back in my flat in Cliftonville.

Afterwards, I lay on my bed and turned on the TV, flicking through the channels. I wasn't watching anything, just thinking back over the day I had just had. After weeks of fantasising about my own business, a car and my own house, it hit me. I was a dreamer, and this was all a pie-in-the-sky idea and the only way I had a chance of actually getting it was by winning the lottery. My stomach churned with disappointment; I was almost grieving over my lost fantasy. I thought about packing up what little stuff I had and just heading home. I must have lain on that bed for hours, staring at the ceiling, punishing myself for daring to dream and being stupid enough to pay the money for the B&B, the travel and the tickets, all for nothing. Money I could not afford.

Then I thought back to the lectures earlier in the day and I realised it was not perhaps a total waste. I did know some things now that I didn't know before. I had already spent the money and everything was all paid for. It would be foolish to waste it. It became a constant battle between my head and my heart. My head telling me, "Be cautious, stick with your day job and try to just make more money, don't gamble everything on this one idea." My heart then saying, "Come on, we can do this. For as long as I'm beating we will always have a chance if we don't give up!"

One of the lecturers I went to hear on that first day talked about having the correct mindset to keep your motivation up. He told us a story about a man walking along the beach when he sees a very successful business owner. The man runs up to the business owner and says, "SIR! Please, I want to be just like you, can you show me how you did it?"

The businessman replies, "First you need to prove to me you are willing to do whatever it takes."

"Yes, yes anything," says the man.

The businessman then points out to sea and says, "Show me how much you want it by walking out in that sea."

"Okay," he says, and he takes his shoes and socks off, pulls his trousers up to his knees and walks into the sea, up to his ankles.

The businessman then shouts, "You're obviously wasting my time, you don't want it."

So the man walks in up to his knees and looks back at the businessman, who stands there, shaking his head as if to say no. The man then walks in up to his chest and shouts back to the businessman.

"Look, surely this proves it."

The businessman continues to shake his head, and points further out. The man walks out even further until he gets to a point where his clothes are pulling him down and the water is up to his neck. Struggling to breathe, he feels a sense of desperation and begins making his way back to shore.

As he sits on the beach the businessman walks over and stands next to him, saying, "To be successful, you have to want success as much as you want to breathe, you have to fight for it, have a sense of desperation for it, but most importantly you have to be very careful when you make your move, to take a breath. You may take a mouthful of water. If so, cough it out and take another breath."

I could understand what the lecturer was trying to say - I had to make myself believe. What have I actually got to lose? Nothing. Nothing at all. The worst thing that could happen is I would go home tomorrow feeling exactly like I did at the end of today. So, feeling slightly more positive I agreed with myself to treat tomorrow as a new day. To go back to Olympia for the final day and give it a proper go. At least I would be able to say that I tried.

I lay there in the dark and began to think back to The Savoy, and how Jason, if it was him, would be spending the night. "I bet he's now having a massage or swimming. No, it's a bit late, maybe he's one of those guys who drinks brandy and reads a book before bed."

I started to wish I was this random person I had never met, but who yet had such a tremendous effect on me. Well, not only me but everyone else there.

Maybe he really was this good and he could point me in the right direction about how to start my business idea. If only I could grab two minutes to speak with him, tell him my idea, and maybe, just maybe, I might make it.

Just Go For It

I checked out of the B&B and headed down to the underground. As I got into the carriage, I noticed everyone in suits. I mean the real expensive kind, not ones that have badges holding their crotches together. People with laptop bags with real laptops in them and money in their wallets. I wanted to be able to have some money in my wallet, how good must that feel? To be able to pick up food and drink for lunch without having to calculate the price to see if you had enough without hearing that awful double beep when your card is declined and everyone around you knows your card just got declined. Then you have to make up this lie, "Oh, I don't know why it's doing that, that's a bit worrying, I've got three grand in there!" Then quickly walk out like you're about to call the bank.

I put my earphones in and started to psych myself up again, just trying to keep my confidence up. As I got closer to Olympia my heart started racing. I got off the train and, just like the day before, the queue was really long, still full of people in expensive suits.

Once the door opened I walked in and kept my earphones in. Just like I was in my own little world. I didn't look around as I did before. I just went straight for what I wanted to see first, which was James Caan's lecture. James Caan is an ex-Dragons' Den investor and has years of recruitment experience under his belt. I raced through all the people and got right to the front. I was so out of my comfort zone. I wasn't even sure why I had sat at the front. I had sat at the back every single time the day before. It made me nervous being so close to the front, but I kept thinking I had nothing to lose, and I had to try. I had to give this all I had and get out of my comfort zone, just like they told us in the confidence lecture the day before. I was going home either way, so I might as well go home with my head held high knowing that I actually gave it a go.

The Dreamer

James Caan walked into the room, his appearance and presence was like that of a celebrity. As you glanced around the room everyone was looking at him with inspiration in their eyes.

Here was someone who could help me get my business going or give me some advice.

James gave a very powerful and inspiring speech. Right before the end he said something that stuck with me; he said, "If you have a business idea, believe in it, believe in yourself, go to the person you are showing it to and have passion, and say, 'I have a fantastic business idea, what do you think?'"

The whole room clapped and cheered as he finished his speech, but I just kept thinking over and over again of his words. I thought back again over my business idea. I really did think it was fantastic, and I had passion. My passion and enthusiasm had brought me here today.

I then got up. I stood there for a while thinking about what I was going to do next. I pulled my folder out of my bag and flicked through it. I needed to show someone. I remembered back to the day before when I had seen the pitching event, so I decided to head there. Maybe I could show one of the investors as he walked to lunch or something, just to see what they thought.

My heart then began beating out of my chest. I was going for it. I'm not going home until someone sees it and tells me what they think.

"Come on, we can do this, just a few seconds of courage," I thought.

I turned and started walking through the middle of the arena with my eyes just fixed on one position, where I had seen the investors and Jason.

I finally found the stage, but the stage itself was empty, a lot of people were still mulling around as if something on stage had just finished. "Maybe I'm too late and they've finished for the day?" I thought as I looked around for any of the investors or Jason.

Then I saw a group of people wearing 'The Golden Touch' logo T-shirts. My hands were probably the sweatiest I've ever felt them, my heart beating faster than I think it had ever before without any exercise. I had no idea what was about to happen but knew that either way it was going to be something I had never experienced before.

They were talking to people and capturing the details on tablets. The longer I stood there the more anticipation built up and the harder it was to go over to them, but before I could do anything someone tapped me on the shoulder. I turned around to be greeted by a young lady with a smiling face.

I immediately burst out, "I've got a fantastic idea for a business, what do you think?" with more enthusiasm than was really needed. I had not planned to do that. I think I frightened her a little with my outburst but the words had just come out, no doubt fuelled by the intense adrenaline pumping through my body. I felt quite stupid, and she could probably tell this from the expression on my face as I held aloft my folder for my idea.

Albeit a little taken back, she politely smiled and said to me, "Let's take a look then." My heart was beating so quickly as she led me to a small table. I began to edge myself onto one of the two bar stools.

She wasn't an investor I had seen on the panel, but someone who had already started up a business and had worked with The Golden Touch in getting her business going. She opened the folder. This was the first stranger to look at my business idea and I was filled with a mixture of emotions. She was seeing my idea for the jobs' website with fresh eyes; this idea I had poured my heart into, that had the potential to help young people who had gone through what I had gone through. I suddenly felt quite protective of it, but at the same time worried that the information wasn't put in a sophisticated enough way for her to take me seriously. I looked at her face to try and see if I could see any negative facial expressions as she read

The Dreamer

through it.

She nodded her head and then looked at me and asked a few questions about the business. What it did, who it was for, why would it work, how it would make money? I had written all that down already, and I showed her. She then turned away and called someone else over, pointing to my folder as she did so. "So is this your business plan?" she said. I had no idea what a business plan was so I just said, "It's more like a few thoughts about my business idea that I've written down, I just need some help getting it started."

Then she turned to me and said, "What a fantastic idea."

Honestly, at that point I could have cried. After the emotions I'd felt over the past couple of days and then to be told that, it was an amazing feeling. Even if the business did not happen, having someone understand, recognise the value and believe in my idea was just incredible. I had never had that before. I was a sewage worker with nothing to my name, had fought for the two days off work to go to a Start Up Business Exhibition full of posh men and women in suits in London, and they thought my idea was good. Maybe I could do this after all.

I was then told about a startup business funding scheme the government had set up to help startups get going. They had a meeting for the very next day and asked if I was interested in attending. I'm sure that you can guess my reply. What an unbelievable feeling. I felt like I had conquered the world. They told me a time I needed to be there, and we said our goodbyes. I walked out of the event with the biggest smile on my face, I was glowing. Surely this is what it feels like to win the lottery!

As I sat on the underground on the way back into central London, my entire body was still pulsing with adrenaline, my hands shaking uncontrollably. I remember recording my hand shaking so I could always remember this moment. It's amazing what your body does. What adrenaline can do to you when its chemistry is rushing through your veins. I couldn't stop smiling. What a day. I tried

Just Go For It

calling Laura and a couple of mates, but they were all at work. They'd have to wait to hear my news.

I had to celebrate. I suddenly realised I hadn't really eaten anything over the past couple of days, so I wandered around London looking for a Weatherspoon's, where I got myself a nice chili con carne and a pint of Stella, my little piece of heaven. I phoned the B&B to ask if I could stay another night.

I hated it there, but I didn't care anymore, I wouldn't be in this situation for long. I've got a BUSINESS! I sat down and enjoyed a tasty dinner for once. It was money I had budgeted for next week but at that very moment I didn't really care. I had worked so hard and just wanted a bit of heaven! At that point in my life heaven was a properly cooked dinner. Even if 'Spoons mostly cook it in the microwave, it still tasted better than 10p noodles. I sat there eating my chili looking around. I started to wonder where people were going out that night. "I wonder what's going on at the Savoy tonight?" I thought to myself. I might go back to have another look before I head back to the B&B, I didn't have much else to do. With my belly full of food and slightly tipsy from a pint - lightweight I know! - I headed back towards The Savoy.

By the time I had finally found it again it was starting to get dark. This time, rather than gleaming in the sunlight, the Savoy sign was lit up brightly, a potent green glow hidden behind the silver shiny letters. The doormen were still there, not the doormen I was used to, these had top hats. I stood at the end of the road gazing down, something pushing me to take a few steps forward for a closer look. I walked slowly down the side pretending to be on the phone so I didn't get asked to leave.

I got to the entrance, phone still pinned to my ear, just trying to get a look at the inside. It looked extremely glamorous. "One day," I said to myself, "one day I will stay here." But then a phrase from the film Gladiator crept in, "Not yet, not yet. Just remember this moment and keep moving forward."

The Dreamer

I woke up the next day with such a great feeling. I was going to Kingston University, which would be the first EVER time for me being inside a uni. But it was in a place I had no idea how to get to. I was running around getting train after train until I finally got to Kingston. I was late and still lost, running up and down the streets asking people for directions, but every time I asked, I was ignored. That's when I found out that some Londoners are just plain rude. Then some kind old gent pointed me in the right direction and I ran there as fast as I could. I got into the university and asked the receptionist where I needed to go, breathless and with a slight panic on my face. She looked on her system, which took an age, then pointed me up the stairs. I sprinted up them and finally found a banner. As I walked down the corridor I could hear someone giving a speech.

Not good, I was late. I peered my head around the corner and could see twenty to thirty people there. The speaker spotted me and waved me in. It was like a large classroom and everyone was right at the front, though me being me, I went straight to the back. I was so hot and sweaty I tried to cool myself down by using leaflets as a makeshift fan, whilst at the same time trying not to make any noise or draw attention to myself.

Jason Currie, Managing Director of The Golden Touch, was standing up and talking. He was saying something about young people starting businesses. I really couldn't concentrate, I was so hot. Then I heard Jason say, "Right, now each of you stand up and tell us a little about yourself, starting with you at the back."

Gulp.

I put my jacket back on and slowly stood up, everyone broke into a round of applause. What the hell was I going to say? I started looking around at people, their eyes all on me, it was so uncomfortable, I started feeling sick. I didn't prepare for this at all. This was the first time I had ever stood up in front of anyone to talk about me or my idea, let alone tell a room of strangers. I was much more comfortable sitting down one-to-one with the lady yesterday. Why couldn't we just do that again?

The clapping then stopped; the silence which lasted only a few seconds felt like hours. I took a deep breath, looked down at the table trying not to make eye contact. The longer I was putting it off, the harder it was going to be. What happened next was the most mumbled speech anyone has ever heard. I felt I wasn't making any sense, I couldn't even remember in my head what I had said after I had just said a few words, but I just wanted to get the words out as quickly as possible and get it over and done with. I thought about what I'd been told about keeping pitches short and simple. No problem there. I explained it was a jobs website aimed at getting young people back to work, as well as a few details about how it would work.

Once I finished, I sat back down and got another round of applause. When I finally looked up I could see people were looking at me, nodding, as if to say, "Good idea." I felt like I had done everything you're not meant to do when speaking to an audience. I wasn't even sure what I had even said or if it made sense. Surely there was no way anybody in that room could have made sense of it. I was just glad it was over and the next person had started speaking already, taking the spotlight off of me.

As the day went on, people would come over during coffee breaks and ask me some questions about my business idea. They wanted to know the same things I'd asked myself – the different ways it would make money, and how I could efficiently reach the people who were my target audience. I showed them my folder and told them about some of my ideas. One woman, Danielle, came over to me. She worked for Jason and wanted to know more about my idea. Being overwhelmed by the whole experience, I couldn't get my words out, and to be honest it probably sounded as though I was drunk. She looked at me like I was some kind of weirdo, probably trying to figure out if there was any chance I actually was drunk. I pushed my folder over to her, and she had a flick through. I kept looking at her face as she read through it, then her eyebrows raised and she looked very impressed. I started to relax a bit and hoped she didn't think I was too crazy. This exchange ended on a positive note. I think she caught a bit of my excitement.

As the day went on we had a few more little breaks. I stood at the back, on my own, while other people chatted to each other. Then this guy came over to me and shook my hand, then told me about his business idea. It was then I realised that all the people who had come to the meeting were in the same boat as me. They all had a great idea for a business and wanted to get it started, but didn't know how. Maybe they were as nervous as me and I just couldn't see it. What is it about these people that makes them look so confident... wait a minute - they *have* confidence. That's something I was definitely lacking.

There were a few more lectures about starting up, then the day came to an end. Aadi, another member of Jason's team, came over to me, pulled up a chair and sat directly in front of me. He asked to take a closer look at my folder and had lots of questions about the business and if I had thought about any names for the business yet? "Not really given it a thought to be honest," I replied. I looked around and suddenly I thought of a name, 'Next Generation Jobs'.

I blurted, "Well, this business is going to be amazing for the next generation. So good in fact I will call it 'Next Generation Jobs'!" He then replied, "What a fantastic name that is."

He then gave me a little more grilling, like something I had witnessed over the past few days. This time, I was much more mentally prepared for it.

I tried to give the best answers I could, telling him I would literally put my heart and soul into making the company a success. If someone of high business stature told me that there was a chance, I would keep working at it until it was a success. He then looked at me with a big smile on his face and asked me if I had a business plan.

I told him that I didn't even know what a business plan was.

He then said, "Well, your new business mentor will be able to help you with that."

I looked confused and didn't really understand, still having the look of 'I don't know how the hell I even got here' on my face.

He then added, "Pending seeing your business plan, YOU'RE IN!"

I was too stunned to respond.

He then went on to say that after I submitted a successful business plan, I would receive a startup business loan of up to £10,000, as well as being assigned a millionaire business mentor. He would arrange for my mentor to meet with me, firstly to go through building a business plan for Next Generation Jobs. I thanked him over and over again, shaking his hand and nodding away like the Churchill dog from the TV adverts. He then walked off to go and speak to other entrepreneurs and hopefully break some good news to them, too.

I sat there, my head spinning at a thousand miles an hour, looking around the room trying to take it all in. Danielle came back over to me and asked if I was okay. "You look like you've seen a ghost," she said.

I was in so much shock I couldn't get any proper words out and just muttered lots of half words and unfinished sentences. She looked at me, bemused, trying to work out what I was saying. The poor woman just kept coming up to me at the wrong time. I finally managed to explain to her what had just happened and that I wasn't drunk or drugged, it was pure shock.

She then laughed and said, "You have a fantastic opportunity here, you have a good business model. With the right guidance and a bit of funding we can get you on your way."

I explained what I had been through to get to this point and this meeting, after which she realised how much it meant to me and why I was in such shock. Danielle then said she would leave me be, to try

The Dreamer

and let it all sink in. She then walked off, while I sat there. This wasn't really happening, surely? It's too good to be true. I was going to wake up in a moment and find myself back in my shitty Cliftonville flat. I looked around and everyone was talking and walking around in a hive of activity. It was at that moment that I truly started to believe in my business idea, and thinking this really could work. I looked around the room and could see not all the people there had the same good news. I was one of the lucky ones. I walked over to Jason who was about to leave and thanked him and for his business giving me the opportunity to shine.

As I sat on the train at London Victoria, back to the reality of working on the roads, gazing out of the window in a total dreamland, my thoughts drifted to the house I wanted to buy one day. I opened my bag and stared at its picture I had printed. Then I put my mp3 back on and started listening to my music again. It was then that I decided to make a promise to myself. I told myself this is a chance of a lifetime, it will never happen again, whatever happens NEVER EVER GIVE UP on it. It is going to be tough and there will be days when I will just want to say 'enough is enough' and pack it all in. DON'T! Keep going. I felt like I had come so far already, yet this was just the beginning.

For the rest of the journey I sat there, with a beaming smile on my face. I must have looked a little deranged, as despite the train being packed, and having an empty seat next to me, nobody took it. Just me, my music playing in my ears, a beaming smile and an A4 picture of a house in my hands. Only one problem. How on Earth do I write a business plan?

Back To Reality

It was dark as I walked to my flat. After navigating my way past some dog shit and dumped rubbish, I finally made it to the building's front door. Climbing up the stairs, I heard a couple of tenants having a huge row. The floors and walls were so thin, it was as if I was in the same room with them. "Home sweet home", I thought. I opened my door and turned on the light, then stood there for a while, looking around, still not able to come to terms with what had happened over the past few days.

I put some sausages in my little deep fat fryer and had a sandwich as I began to write down the next steps. What sort of things the funding could be used for, the stuff I was going to need.

Over the next few days, I would go to the internet cafe after work and start researching business plans. I was eager and impatient, I wanted to get things going ASAP. I found a good example online and started to build mine. I had a USB stick that I had managed to pinch from work and I would save the business plan on it each day. I had discovered it was similar to what I had already done with my thoughts, which I'd written down in my folder. It was just a case of rewriting it to look more professional. I also needed to add a section that I didn't have already, about future forecasts and future profits. This is where I became very stuck. I didn't have a clue about pricing or what my website would be selling. What I had planned on was for the website to have Google AdSense and to make the revenue from that. Google AdSense is an advertising platform that allows adverts to be shown on the website, and you are paid every time someone clicks on it.

I realised that I had to find other ways of making money from it. I searched similar websites and found other ways, such as charging for job postings. But it was still difficult to figure out how much I should charge for the services offered. I read a blog post written by a business owner who said writing a business plan is someone's best guess at how the business will pan out, it's a plan of what will be happening in the future. But as everyone knows, nothing ever goes to plan.

Having a few minutes left at the end of my hour's hire of the computer at the internet café, I thought I would start looking at the high end of life and what it would be like if I became a millionaire from my business. The Savoy was straight on my wish list, their website was as glamorous as the outside of the hotel. One night next weekend, what would that cost? £1200… yeah that will be definitely something for when I'm a millionaire, that's like a few months' rent. Next was the Maldives, crystal clear seas and rooms that were on stilts over the sea. One place I found was called Velassaru; the promo video had some really chilled music as it flashed around the fancy hotel. Imagine sitting on that beach or in the water villa where you can sit on the toilet and look through the floor at the fish swimming around beneath you. And how would I get there if I was a successful business owner? First class of course! Typing in 'First class', autofill then suggested First Class Fly Emirates. There was a video of a very successful couple sitting on an A380, First Class, champagne all the way, sitting in a booth on the plane. It looked out of this world… then they said they had booked a shower! A shower on a plane, that's just crazy. I just wanted that to be me on the way to the Maldives.

But I said, NOT YET, NOT YET. First things first. I will have to get myself back home and try to get some sleep and be ready for another gruelling day at work.

It was still freezing cold all the time, but during those weeks I was working with tarmac. So with all the physical activity that involved - jumping on the back of the lorry, shovelling off tons and tons of the stuff into wheelbarrows, then jumping down and running it over to my boss who would be laying it - at least I was warm. In the summer the back of the lorry would get so hot you could fry an egg on the floor where the tarmac had been.

Sometimes I was allowed to take the van home. My boss wasn't keen on the idea because of the area, but sometimes we didn't have a choice because of the logistics of it all.

One night I heard some loud noises coming from outside my flat. I looked out of the window and saw someone on the back of the pick-up truck that my boss had lent me. He'd told me to guard it with my life. Then I saw another figure standing by the side. They were trying to break into the lockbox that was on the back and which held all our tools. I ran down, and once they saw me coming out from the front door, they jumped down and ran off. I went over to look at the back of the van and saw that the bastards had broken the side of the box to try and get in. It was so badly damaged I would have to tell my boss in the morning, which I did. His response was to tell me that I couldn't take the van home anymore, as he didn't want to risk anything being stolen. A few weeks before this someone had broken into the van while we were working on another street in Cliftonville, and they'd stolen my wallet and phone while I was working.

I had to get out of that place. I had to try harder and work faster to make sure this business was a success so I could finally have my own home. A house I could call my own, that didn't have cat and dog shit on the doorstep or people screaming at each other halfway through the night. Somewhere I could feel safe, somewhere I could leave my belongings which wouldn't get smashed up for a laugh.

I told myself that it was a stopgap, a stepping stone to bigger and better things, I just had to ride it out for now.

I asked my boss if there was any overtime going, and I managed to get a few extra hours. I was trying to save as much money as I could. Christmas was round the corner and Laura was coming down to spend Christmas with me in the flat. So I worked late in the evenings and some weekends on another contract where we worked in the sewers. But as soon as the money came into my bank the creditors would get their hands on it and it would be gone. I was still trying to take cash from the ATM before they could get their mitts on it all. I knew I would be getting deeper in debt with the start-up loan, but that was my way out. That was going to be the way I could pay back these bills and not have to quickly walk to the ATM at midnight to withdraw cash so I could live.

I had met Laura through running, three years before I'd joined the Royal Marines. Having asthma at a young age I had to wait four years for it to come off my medical records so I could join the Royal Marines. I had a friend who was about to join the army as a nurse, so she and I would train together to keep fit. I fancied her too, which was a bit of extra motivation to go running. Then one day she said that a friend of hers would like to come along. This was Laura.

For three years we were inseparable, but when I joined the Marines she moved to London to live with her auntie. She got a job and worked on the tills at Tesco, who don't allow mobile phones in the workplace. So she would put hers in her sock, setting it on vibrate. We had a little code for if either of us was in trouble; if I needed her I would ring and ring, she'd feel the vibration and then get someone to cover the till so she could call me.

I hadn't had a proper girlfriend before, so Laura literally was my first love, and I assumed that we were going to be together forever, so after a while I started taking it for granted that she would always be there for me.

And then I'd joined the Marines with the separation making things worse, and I'd eventually become so worried about always hearing about her 'friend' that I decided to quit.

After handing in my notice with the Marines it was six months before I got a job.

By the time Christmas arrived, I'd bought a few extra home comforts. I'd also plugged up the cracks in the windows to stop the draft, and completely closed off the bedroom so the smell of mould didn't invade the entire flat. I'd also acquired a microwave. All I wanted to do was to have the best possible Christmas with Laura. I was given a turkey from a company we had a contract with, but I still didn't have any way of cooking it as it was far too big to put into the microwave - if you could even cook it that way? Mr Bean cooked a turkey in the microwave... yeah maybe it wasn't such a good idea. I did get hold of a Christmas tree though, but the few decorations I could afford made it look quite bare and was pretty laughable. I did the front room up the best I could to make it feel a bit homely. I didn't have much to offer, but it was everything I had.

Laura arrived. She'd brought with her some cooked sliced turkey, so at least we had a bit of turkey for Christmas, albeit in sandwiches made by her auntie; still, a nice touch. I'd put £20 on my electric key and saved it so we could have the heating on all day. The halogen lamps were amazing, and we could just lay around in our pj's and enjoy it. At mid-day I checked the meter and we'd already used up half of it! I hadn't realised that electric on a key was so expensive.

We exchanged presents, but I could only get a token gift for her. I felt so ashamed of myself. I didn't feel like a real man. In my mind, a real man is meant to provide for his girl. I told her that it wouldn't be like this for long, that I would make my business a success and I would be a millionaire so I could buy us a lovely house and provide for her. She smiled and tried to understand, but it didn't stop me feeling like a total failure.

After Christmas, Laura went back up to London. I was back on my own again, working flat out. I would buy as many motivational films as I could.

Rocky, The Pursuit of Happiness, Wall Street. They would help me to feel inspired. I knew they were characters in films, but some of them, like The Pursuit of Happiness, were based on true stories. The Pursuit of Happiness is about a man who didn't have anything but still managed to provide a home for his child, who loved him for it.

The Dreamer

These were all played on a video/TV combo. Videos were being sold down the high street for next to nothing, practically giving them away. Waste not, want not!

I also bought a few books, reading about successful business owners who had started from absolutely nothing and went on to build empires. Like the lady who started Specsavers and who, even though she was a multi-millionaire, would still ride her bike to work.

There was a good one from Dale Carnegie, How to Win Friends and Influence People. The information in this book has helped me throughout my life. Things like being a good listener and not to compare stories when someone is trying to tell you theirs - just listen and people will start to appreciate you. Maybe this would help me get a few friends on the way.

All Go And No Show

I continued trying to finish my business plan, bit by bit. After doing a bit of research, I thought £9.99 would be a good price for jobs to be listed. I was going to do sales calls to businesses in the area and try to get some jobs listed, then I could advertise the hell out of them and try to get as many applications for each job as I could. Hopefully, news would spread about Next Generation Jobs and more people would like to advertise on it.

When I finally finished the business plan, spending hours and long nights down the internet café, I sent it to The Golden Touch. I got an email back from Aadi saying he was just about to set up a meeting with my mentor to polish it, but after reading it through, a meeting was obviously not needed. I was happy with that. I then received a further email. My business plan had been accepted; they reckoned I'd need £5,000, and my start-up loan funds would be on their way to me. I must have read that email a hundred times. I just needed a business bank account. My credit rating was so bad I was actually scared to look on any credit rating website through fear they'd blacklisted me, or some business was trying to take me to court.

I had no choice but to just apply for a business bank account. Filling in the details was exciting and nerve-wracking. Then came the submit button... it had worked, and Next Generation Jobs now had its own business bank account! WOW, what a step that was. The balance read £0, but obviously that wouldn't be for long, my funds were on their way.

I checked the bank account every day, waiting for my money to be put in, it was a very nervous time. Then one day I checked, and there it was. I couldn't believe it, £5,000. I had the funds to start my little baby. That's what it felt like, it felt like I now had a child and had to nurture and care for it.

I had already worked out how I would spend the funding. I had a recommendation from a friend of mine for an excellent web designer. I didn't know anything about web design, so I emailed the designer and asked if he could create my website. I had so many ideas, I wanted to revolutionise the online job portal. There was going to be a section for courses as well as jobs - if jobs could be advertised so could training courses to help applicants get that role. There was going to be a section for online interviews via webcams, you could book a slot via the website. I also had an idea to use business cards, but for individual people. So if you walked past a window with a job offer displayed you could walk in and hand over your card. This would have all your details as well as an NFC (Near-Field Communication) in the card so if you touched it to the back of a phone, it would take the person hiring to your own personal job page. Don't have NFC on your phone? No problem, there will also be a QR code on the card to scan. This way every job candidate could have their individual website to show off their skills. This was going to be called an eCV (Electronic Curriculum Vitae); past employers could leave reviews about the candidate's experience. My ideas were the result of a combination of market research and some original thinking.

There was also going to be a health and fitness blog where I could get bloggers to post about how to stay active and refreshed during the endless days of applying for hundreds of jobs and not getting a reply.

The web designer came back with a quote of £10,000. I wasn't given that much so I had to cut out a few of the extra goodies I wanted to put on the site. The web designer explained to me that it is sometimes best to bring out new developments for the website gradually. I agreed. I had no choice. The ideas would have to be put on the back burner for a bit and I would just concentrate on job postings.

I was sent a few websites for design ideas, with the suggestion that he would build something similar. It was still going to use up 80% of my money. I hadn't realised a website build was so expensive and asked him why it cost so much. He gave me a load of technical jargon which confused the hell out of me. At the end of the day he was recommended to me, so I just had to trust him. Besides, I didn't know anywhere else to find someone to build a website.

I asked for a few features to be included, but they still cost the moon.

He told me he saw no difficulties, and it would be ready in three months. I wasn't expecting it to take that long, but as a non-tech guy I suppose I was a little naïve. I just tried to look at the positives, I now had three months to make sure everything was perfect. As people had told me, "Failure to prepare is to prepare to fail." So, after picking a good-looking design, I sent the money over and just had to wait.

Next on the list was a laptop. I couldn't keep walking to the internet café and working from there. So I went out laptop shopping, stopping off at computer stores in the work van when I had asked my boss if I could drive the van to the shops, it needed to be done. There was a nice cheap one I found for only a few hundred pounds. Argos were selling dongles so you could connect to the internet, so I bought one of them as well.

After getting home from work I would have a lukewarm bath and lay on the mattress on the floor in my front room, working away.

I looked at my emails and had received my first invitation to a mentoring session, which was to be held in London. I caught the bus that weekend and got a cheap suit from Primark. It was a vast improvement from the badge-pinned trousers I used to wear. You can really look good for just a few pounds in there, a new pair of trousers and a nice new tie with a jacket. It made all the difference; and to me, I felt good.

I went up to London in my new suit and with a laptop FINALLY in my laptop bag. London was the place to be. When you get off that train and walk out from London Victoria it's a busy place, but I just love the buzz of it all.

I walked into a very prestigious-looking building and told the receptionist I was there to see my mentor from The Golden Touch. I was asked for my name. "Dave Brett of Next Generation Jobs."

"Oh yes Mr Brett, they are expecting you." I was then directed to a floor of the building where I saw other people dressed up and hanging around chatting in the halls, carrying their laptop bags. I wasn't jealous this time as I knew mine actually had a laptop in it. They were also very young, so I assumed that they were other mentees in the same mentoring session as me. We chatted for a bit about their businesses. One guy was there with a coin and he said it was going to be the future, "This coin is not worth anything, but what it represents is the future of currency." I asked him, "What's it called?" He replied, "Bitcoin. I have all my worth in Bitcoin and I'm building a platform for others to purchase it. The worth of Bitcoin goes up and down but one day this will take over from that old paper money in your pocket, you should come on my platform and put some money in." I was in the same room as someone who understood Bitcoin. He was building a website for buying and selling Bitcoins, and there was something about this guy's energy that made me trust my instincts that he was onto something.

A few months after this conversation I went on his website and set up my account to get £100 worth and completely forgot about it. Then a few years ago when Bitcoin's price went to the moon I remembered about this and checked my account to see how much it was worth... I had forgotten to actually buy some, the £100 was still in the account uninvested! At the time of writing this book a single Bitcoin had reached the heady heights of £70k in value. Oh well, you win some, you lose some.

Others were there with some really good ideas too. There was a guy with dyslexia, and he was building an app to help people. It had a screen to put over words and you could swipe through the different colours to make it easier to see the words. What a brilliant idea. This idea has since been adopted by many different writing apps.

Then the big doors at the end of the corridor opened to where the mentoring session would be held. Standing there was a woman dressed in a suit and smiling broadly. She invited me in and introduced herself as Mercedes, my new business mentor, dressed in a very nice pinstripe suit. You could see from the way she presented herself that she was extremely confident, with an aura that was apparent to everyone in the room.

I sat down and got my notepad out, I was there with about ten other people, these were the people I had just met in the corridor. All looking as excited as me, and all had that Rocky eye of the tiger.

We all sat taking notes as Mercedes gave us some amazing advice. But it wasn't just that, she gave everyone in the room the feeling that you could conquer the world if you wanted to. You just sat there feeling very special and oozing with confidence. I didn't even understand what mentoring was, to be honest. I had imagined I would be told what and how to run my business, that they would be my boss, as such. But it wasn't like that at all. It's more like having your own tutor. Someone who's been there and seen most of what happens in business. Passing over essential knowledge to you, so you don't fall into the same traps as they did. I'm a strong believer in the power of training and mentoring. If you want to be successful in business, you should never fall into the trap of believing your education journey is over. I put this same passion into the training section of my jobs' website, and because of that, I think it helped me build a better product.

As I sat there I could feel my confidence growing. I was joining in with conversations and speaking in front of the people in the room. I was absolutely loving it. This wasn't normally me; I would usually keep quiet in a room full of people, but my confidence in myself and my business was growing. We then sat down for a little one-to-one about how the business was going and she gave me some excellent advice. Research this, make sure you know about this, make sure you contact businesses to get some feelers, get a press release drawn up. It was all brilliant information.

When the mentoring session finished, I dished out my brand-new business cards to everyone there and shook their hands. I had a notebook full of advice given to me by Mercedes. I took as much information away as I could, and I had notes on press releases and marketing.

It was so strange to even think about the Press. Why would the press be interested in me? I've only started up a job website for young people! I asked Mercedes this and she told me it was a human-interest story. I was helping young people, and I had been there and done it - I had been laid off before and was out of work for six months and struggling like hell to get a job - but it's so hard to get a start anywhere when you are young, inexperienced and without qualifications.

That's why I know what the problem is, and I'm fixing it. It was good to have someone in my corner, backing me up with what I was doing, finding the positives in every situation. That's something I learned very well from Mercedes, to get the best out of every dark and gloomy moment.

After three months of planning for the launch and waiting for the website, I finally got an email saying the website was ready. I was at work at the time, but I had a new phone so I could read my emails. I didn't want to see the website on my phone, so I impatiently waited for the day to finish so I could rush home to see it. I had my dongle for connection to the internet but I had to pay a fortune to use it. A lot more than £1 an hour at the internet cafe, but at least I didn't have to walk down there and could save all the information on my laptop. But it was the slowest internet in the history of this planet. It's the biggest test of any person when you click on a link and you can see the bar start loading across the screen, but it's going slower and slower, then when it's near the end, stops completely.

It finally came up, and all of the excitement I was feeling evaporated, and my heart sank. This was not my website, this was not what I'd asked for, this wasn't even half a job. I honestly thought the website was still loading at one point, but it had, the website was that bad. I started to click on the links and throughout the website I found I was faced with error 404. I had no idea what error 404 was, but I knew it probably wasn't good.

My spelling is absolutely shocking at best, but even I was finding spelling mistakes in most of the text. Broken links, missing text and missing pages were just some of the other problems on this so-called website.

I tried the candidate registration process.

I managed to sign up, but no email was sent through so I could complete the registration and apply for jobs. It wouldn't have been a problem if my website was just a small part of my business, but my website WAS my business, everything depended on my website being perfect. How could I get people to trust my services if even I didn't trust the tool I was offering? I was livid. I had taken a huge gamble on something that shouldn't have been a gamble. I thought this guy was a sure thing and the website he would make for me would be my dream website. I had put 80% of my startup money on this and ended up with something that seemed to have been constructed by a three-year-old.

For weeks and weeks I battled with this guy over trying to sort out the problems. I had no access to changing hardly anything at the back end, so I couldn't even change the spelling mistakes. At first, when I was given the admin login details for the site, I couldn't even upload my logo. To make matters worse, the guy was completely slack in replying to my emails, often taking three days to give an answer. I didn't have any other contact details for him so I would get frustrated when I didn't get a reply and wondered if I had made the email too aggressive. Maybe I asked for too much? I really didn't know.

Eventually he literally became unreachable and didn't respond to any emails at all. I was starting to lose my time and money and not getting anywhere. I had no option but to try and work with the website as much as I could.

The admin side of the website worked to a point, and I could at least change a few things. I found a page that was full of code, it looked like something from The Matrix. I would by trial and error replace texts on the back end of the website to see if it would change anything. I managed to change the spelling mistakes, but there were still a lot of mistakes I couldn't fix and, due to my poor spelling, things I thought looked right but actually weren't.

By this point I had set up my marketing campaigns and had advertised on social media. I look back now and cringe. Some of the things I used in my first set of advertising were, and there are no other words for it, completely shit.

I remember researching online and collecting email addresses for businesses and putting all these addresses in the "To" section of the email, so everyone I had sent them to could see it was a generic email to everyone. I remember getting a very sarcastic response from a guy saying, "Make sure you blind copy next time idiot!" That was a learning curve.

I would phone companies whenever I had time, offering them our services and just genuinely getting the word out there about my new business. That was one of the most difficult things that I had ever done and something I have never come to enjoy. Telemarketing to me is one of the hardest and most aggravating things. At least when you are face to face with someone in a meeting you can shake their hand and look into their eyes to show someone you are what you say you are. I did start to make some progress though and was getting clients interested and posting jobs. Then one day I was on the phone with a client during my break at work and he told me he had typed in the web address but nothing was coming up. I said that was impossible, I had seen the website a few hours before the phone call. It was a brand-new website, I assured him. He tried the URL again and the same thing happened.

I made up some story and told him that I forgot that the web designer would be making improvements to the site, so it's off-line. I hung up and tried the website on my mobile. Nothing. I was at work at the time and had to wait five of the longest hours of my life to get home. When I finally did I rushed in and logged on the slowest internet on the face of the earth, then waited for my site to load. Still nothing. I thought it could be my internet so I checked another site. It loaded up straight away. It actually loaded the other website faster than ever, so there wasn't anything wrong with the dongle and it was actually faster than it had been before.

I started to panic. I checked my emails, but still nothing from my web designer. My heart racing, I searched online for my web designer's details and managed to find a phone number. I called it but no one picked up. I had an address too, but it was miles away, and I didn't have any transport to get there.

I had no other choice but to call in sick for the rest of the week. I was self-employed and didn't get any wages for time off, but I risked losing the clients and the goodwill that I had already built up. I endlessly searched the web to try and find ways to get my site back. I spent days and nights sitting there trying to find a solution, but it was all in vain.

The web designer had simply pulled the website offline, and I couldn't get hold of him through any means. I contacted my friend and told him what had happened. He was in shock and apologised for recommending him. He told me he'd used him before and didn't have any problems.

I just had to come to terms with the fact that this supposedly trustworthy and professional web designer, who came extremely recommended, had run off with my money and my website too. The thing that worried me the most was what if he takes my idea and starts up a website himself, exactly like the one I wanted to start? He's got all my ideas; it was like someone had run off with my child. I felt so lost.

As I was taking days off all the time, I fell out with my boss who then would only give me a few days' work a week as I had become unreliable, and this meant that I wasn't getting paid a full week's wage. It didn't look good for him and his business as I was meant to be going to jobs he had contracts for, but I wasn't turning up. I was actually pretty lucky he didn't stop giving me work altogether.

I now had lots of money going out and hardly any coming in. I was starting to run out of money extremely quickly. This really hit home when I went to the ATM on the Friday morning to withdraw £10… and it was refused. I had gone over my agreed overdraft again. My wages had gone in and it didn't even touch the sides. My pay didn't even take me out of my unauthorised overdraft. I looked into my wallet and had that all too familiar feeling. I had £2 to live on until next Friday, a week away. I went home and searched the flat for all the 2ps and 1ps I could find, then walked down to the nearest coin sorter and prayed I had £10 for the weekend. I had £12. I was so lucky, but from now on I had to be so careful with my money.

For the next three months, I was forced to budget on £2 a day for food and drink. I had to find the bargains again. Space Raiders, 10p noodles and maybe a pot noodle if I was really having a good day. It was a good experience really because I found that if you buy the own brands, most of the food has a hell of a lot more flavour than the more expensive name brands.

One day I found myself in Iceland, and everything was £1, but £1 was half my daily budget. I was walking around the shop with a carrier bag of shopping that I'd bought in Morrison's, including some washing-up liquid. The bag slipped from my hand, and the washing-up liquid I had bought for 40p to try and wash my clothes with, spilt all over the floor. A woman turned and looked at me and gave me a look like she knew I was having a bad time. I was so embarrassed, not only because of that happening, but because of the brand it was, everyone could see I was skint, everything in my bags was Morrison's own brand.

As I knelt down to put the other stuff back in the bag, I looked up and could see everyone was staring at me. It was right by the tills, so everyone was there waiting, and I was their entertainment. I'd had enough and just left the cheap washing-up liquid there on the floor, along with the microwavable pizza I was going to buy as a treat. I walked from the store feeling such shame, wondering how my life had come to this.

It hadn't been that long ago when I had everything going for me. I felt so stupid for putting everything I had into the website; all my trust, and all my money. It was just so unfair how someone could do such a thing and leave you living like this. I was meant to be buying a house and was going to be a millionaire on the way to the Maldives, but now I was reduced to this.

When I got home I phoned Laura, but she was at work. I used our code and kept ringing her and she ran off her till to answer me. I was in tears down the phone and just wanted her to come and see me.

She did just that and came down that very weekend. She was skint too having put all her money into driving lessons and her test. But she had managed to borrow some money from her auntie to come and see me in a car she had borrowed.

We walked along the seafront and chatted over things. We saw some dogs playing on the beach and she told me she loved animals. I suggested we could go to see some at the zoo. She laughed at my idea as neither of us had any money whatsoever and just getting into the zoo is extremely expensive.

I remembered, years before, someone had told me about a hidden footpath that actually went over the local zoo. So we got in the car and drove to this random location and I told her I was going to surprise her. We walked along the roadside and saw a sign buried in the bushes: 'Public Footpath'. It was true, there was a path that went

The Dreamer

over the zoo, but it looked like it hadn't been used in years. After walking past all the overgrown shrubs we came to a footbridge. When we went over it you could see the zoo and all the people walking around. We stood there for a while at a distance trying to see if we could make out any animals.

The path went on a bit further, so we walked down and found another footbridge. This one was all sealed up. The zoo obviously didn't want people to see what was behind it. We managed to peek through a tiny crack and could see some elephants. The other side of the bridge was completely impassable, but you had an amazing view of the elephants' enclosure because the panel that was meant to be hiding the view had blown over. We then saw an elephant walking towards us. I remember feeling really sad. I had nothing to offer Laura except a sneak view through the panels and by luck a panel that had blown over. But in that moment I think she sensed it. She pulled me close and said, "This is perfect, thank you."

To The Rescue

I left the whole business idea alone for a while and didn't talk to anyone about it. I was thinking about walking away from the whole thing. I wasn't getting anywhere and was now financially worse off than I was to start with. Plus, I was risking my day job by taking so much time off. Soon the work would no longer be there for me if I couldn't work when they needed me to. I felt so embarrassed and ashamed. At any chance I got I went back to working in the sewers as much as I could for a bit of overtime, hoping the memories of the last few months would disappear. Very naïve I know, but it felt like a bad dream, and I just wanted out.

One day I was on site with a workmate and we finished early. We came back through Margate before going back to the yard as my workmate wanted to pick up a train ticket. As I sat in the train station, I looked on my phone and saw a text from my mum saying, "I will always love you, be good." This was odd. My mum didn't normally text me; we very rarely spoke. My little sister used to text me stupid things like that, from my mum's phone, to wind me up, and I would always know it was her. But this time, for some reason, something told me it was different. Something told me to text her back. I replied, "Shut up, you soppy woman," and she wrote back, "I mean it alright; I love you and be good."

It hit me in the back of my throat, and I just felt as though something wasn't right. I got an overwhelming feeling to go to her. So I told my workmate what was going on and he drove me to my mum's.

I still knew where the spare key was, and as I walked through the front door, I started shouting; but it was all very quiet, even their two dogs weren't there. I had all my work clothes on and my boots and didn't want to walk upstairs, so I called up but didn't hear anything

The Dreamer

back.

I heard lots of sirens coming from the park that was down the road, so I ran down, thinking maybe she had taken the dogs for a walk.

As I got to the park I could see some people gathered around someone lying on the floor. Then two dogs were barking. Suddenly the two dogs came running over to me, they were my mum's and stepdad's. Bit weird to think back now, but they definitely came behind me and it felt like they started pushing me towards the person on the ground. So I ran over, the dogs leading the way.

When I got there, the paramedics were already there and my mum was lying unconscious on the ground. I was told to try and hold the dogs back as they were sitting on my mum trying to stop anyone getting close to her. I shouted, "That's my mum!" I grabbed the dogs and held them back while the paramedics tried to resuscitate her. My stepdad worked just around the corner, so I phoned him and told him what was going on. He said he'd be there straight away.

The paramedics then said they had a pulse and brought over a stretcher. By the time they had walked her to the other side of the park where the ambulance was, my stepdad had arrived. He went with her in the ambulance but there wasn't any room for me. I saw it drive off, but I was left holding the two dogs on leads. By this time everyone had come down from the street to see what was going on. My mum's neighbour was there and said, "I can look after the dogs for you, if you want to go to the hospital." I didn't need asking twice. I know we hadn't spoken in so long and had fallen out, but at the end of the day you only get one mum.

I couldn't afford a pot noodle at the time, let alone my own car or public transport, and my workmate had gone home. So I got some of my old trainers out from a bag of stuff that I'd got from the work van, and ran to the hospital.

I was still a decent runner from when I was training to be a Royal Marine. The ambulance went around the top of the road and had to come back on itself. I took a shortcut and ran straight through; I even jumped a few fences and ran through some back gardens. I was then on the main road and the ambulance came past me, now only two miles from the hospital. I managed to keep up with the ambulance as it weaved through the traffic. Then I overtook it while it got stuck in traffic, and I still had another shortcut that led straight to the hospital.

I got there so quickly the hospital didn't even know she had arrived.

When I was allowed to, I walked in and found my mum connected to loads of machines, surrounded by doctors. She was still unconscious and it was plain to see that the doctors looked very concerned. We were then asked to wait outside while they tried to bring her round.

As I sat in the waiting room with my stepdad, I started thinking back to a time when I was little. I was around six or seven years old and had come home from school. As I walked up the pathway, I heard lots of screaming and I saw a suitcase being thrown out onto the front garden, with my mum's clothes in it.

I went into the house and saw my mum and dad screaming at each other. My dad's hands were around my mum's neck. Frightened, I ran into the front room, when the lights suddenly went out. My dad had ripped all the fuses out of the fuse box. He had grabbed a knife and went around the house smashing everything up. He then went upstairs, knife still in hand, and started slashing and stabbing at the brand-new bed, the bed that my mum had scrimped and saved to buy. He tore it to pieces, cutting and ripping at the fabric with the knife.

I stayed in the front room scared and unsure what to do. I just froze. My older sister came home and sat with me for a bit downstairs before going up to see what was going on. My mum quickly gave her some matches, she came back down and lit four candles in a candle holder so we could see in the dark. My mum screamed at her to go next door and call the police as my dad had now smashed the phone.

As my sister began heading for the door, my dad threw my mum to the floor and pulled my sister to the ground, by her skirt. I just stood there, completely helpless, not knowing what to do. I couldn't think. I couldn't move.

The next thing I remember is being held by a police officer and going to a hotel.

It was always like this as far back as I can remember with my real dad. He was asleep on the sofa most days because he didn't have a job. One time, my sister and I were desperate to play on the Super Nintendo my mum had just bought us. It was the new thing out and was major in terms of revolutionary gaming. Whilst my mum didn't have much money, she would spend what she had on us. She had saved for months to buy us that Super Nintendo. We never expected one but she always wanted the best for us. We excitedly switched it on and began playing Mario Brothers. With our eyes glued to the TV and our hands wrapped around the shiny new controllers, we made our way through the first level. This was incredible. I got so excited when I completed the second level that I woke dad up. We both breathed in knowing this was not good. He got up and drove his foot into the console, smashing it to pieces.

After the day that the police took us away, I never saw or heard from him again. Not even a birthday card. It didn't bother me. I preferred him not being in our life. Things were better. No man should ever put his hands on a woman, or treat his family the way he did, and I will never forgive him for it.

My mum then looked after my sister and me on her own, building the house my dad had left to rot into something rather special. She worked three jobs caring for people and we would have to come with her to work most times as she couldn't afford childcare. So we would either sit in the car and wait for her to finish, or sometimes, if she asked the old people, they would let us come in and sit in the front room to watch the telly. Not a bad time, as we frequently got biscuits and squash from the extremely nice old ladies and gentlemen.

My mind came back to the present when, after what felt like an eternity, the doctor came over to update us on what was going on. He told us how she was now in a stable condition and should make it through. He then told me she'd had a fit that may have been brought on by a stroke. She'd had a few major ones in the ambulance on the way to hospital too, one of which nearly killed her.

I had known when I got her message that something wasn't right, she must have known something was up and texted me just in case anything happened to her. Isn't it funny how our gut sometimes knows more than our mind? I always trust my gut, every single time.

I went back to mum's house after the hospital with my stepdad and uncle and auntie, who had driven up from Devon as soon as they had found out. I was still in shock, but tried to keep a brave face when I was around everyone. But when they went to bed I broke down in the kitchen. I lay on the floor, half-drunk staring up at the light, going over everything and wondering how it went so wrong. I kept going over all that had happened - with my business, the web designer, my flat, my dreams and now my mum. It felt like it was all falling apart. I couldn't keep anything together. I didn't know who to turn to and felt very alone. I felt like I had nobody I could speak to or reach out to.

I don't know why, but it was at that moment I thought back to the encouragement my business mentor had provided. I got up and started writing an email to Mercedes on mum's computer, telling her all about the disaster I'd had with my business, and found myself telling her everything that had happened. How ashamed and embarrassed I was. I kept the email purely focused on the business and didn't mention my mum, but just getting everything off my chest about the business made me feel immediately better.

I woke up the next day and Mercedes had sent me the most motivational and inspirational email I have ever received or seen to date. It reminded me of some of the comments that the trainer, Mickey, in the film Rocky often says, like "Get up ya bum! I didn't hear no bell!"

If At First You Don't Succeed

I went up to see my mum as often as I could at the hospital. They did an MRI scan and found what they had suspected. She'd had a minor stroke which had caused the fits.

I remember coming up to see her one time and she was now conscious, but clearly still not with it. She would repeat things over and over again, not remembering what she had said and done. It was incredibly sad. I said to her, "What you need is a nice holiday, why don't you get away?" She said, "I don't have the money to go away, I love holidays and flying. I haven't been on a plane in years." So I decided to make her a promise. "Once I get this business up and running and doing well financially again, I'm going to take you away on holiday." I don't think she ever really believed me, or couldn't remember.

But I remembered the story of the man walking in the sea and struggling to breathe; fighting for each breath was the way to survive. The way to succeed. That was what I needed to do now, so back to the hell hole flat and back to it!

With my motivation fired back up, I started to think about ways to get out of this mess, one step at a time. Even if it's baby steps at least it's still going forward. The incident with my mum had refuelled a fire within me, and Mercedes' email got me back in the right frame of mind. Anyone can lie down and stay down, but a winner will get back up and will be that much harder to knock down next time. I started to write out a little timeline so I could tick off the things as I got back on track.

First thing was to sort out a website. Without one I didn't have a business. It was essential that I had full control over it, that someone else couldn't destroy it. The only person I could think of who I could truly rely on was me. So, over the next few weeks, I worked my

The Dreamer

heart and soul out at work to get back into my boss's good books, which led me to get full weeks of work back again. This meant more money.

As for the website, the only way forward was to build it myself. The problem with that was that I knew absolutely nothing about coding or even making a website online. I sat at home for nights on end and every weekend, researching everything about building websites. My knowledge was minimal at best - I had to learn everything from scratch. I learned to code so I could understand what the scripts did and retain full control over everything. The time had passed when I was going to let people walk over me. From then on I was going to treat everyone with suspicion, and if I needed something from them, then I was going to research as much as possible and negotiate to drive the price as low as I could. Business is business at the end of the day.

I found a place where I could go after work. I learnt about coding and website building. It was like a back street class for beginners and cheap, the guy treated the class as more of a hobby and enjoyed teaching others the value of computer knowledge. A job search website wasn't a simple task that could be done using templates that many companies advertised. It needed to be built using one of the content management systems (CMS) available. I soaked up everything that I was taught, and then built up enough skills to finally start working on the website from my flat, working until 2am most nights. Then getting up at 6am for work, and hand-digging three-meter holes in the ground to find a broken sewer pipe, or laying twenty to thirty tons of tarmac by hand a day. That was my life for quite a few weeks, my normal working day. Unsurprisingly, I was exhausted all the time.

I was fed up too. Screw the creditors. I had added to my home comforts and got myself a PlayStation. I'm an avid Chelsea football club fan and had to buy FIFA. The thing is, it's so easy to glance over at your PlayStation controller and think 'just one game' and abandon the efforts on what I really needed to focus on, so I pinned the picture of my dream house above the TV. Every time I put it on, I would be reminded that by playing the game, rather than working, the longer I would have to wait to start my business and hopefully change my life for the better. It worked too, as every time I turned on the TV I felt a burning feeling from the picture that I couldn't shake off, and I ended up flipping the laptop back open to carry on working.

I always searched for startup business advice online. I found a website called PeoplePerHour which had excellent cheap freelancers who could help with any, and all, aspects of starting, creating and running a business. There was also another website I used time and time again, called Fiverr.

Basically, people would put up their services, offering small odd-jobs that were all priced at $5 (around £3). You could have a logo designed, for example, or have someone convert your marketing material into a different colour or graphic. They were amazing sites and opened up a whole new world of resources. When I was up and running I now knew exactly where I would hire someone to do my dreaded sales calls for me.

I started getting emails from The Golden Touch about my next mentoring sessions, which were scheduled during work hours. I sat down with my boss and had a chat with him. I explained to him that I wanted to start my own business and needed the time off. But not to think I was having the time off because I didn't want my job, but because I wanted my own home one day. He understood me in the end; I think it was because he could relate back to when he was starting up his own business.

But that didn't stop the lads on site from having cheeky digs all day. "You?! What makes you think you can do that? Millionaire? Look at where you live," laughing excessively at me. If a boxer was told he would lose a fight, I'm pretty sure he would walk into that ring and lose. I don't know why people always have to try and piss on your dreams. Why don't they try to spur you on?

I began to go to my mentoring sessions, but I had missed a few when I was feeling low so had to catch up. Each session was based on a different aspect of business: marketing, PR, sales, and branding. Everything was tailored around trying to give you the tools to help you along your business venture. Every mentoring session I had felt like another step up the business ladder. I took as many notes as I possibly could. At the end of some of these sessions Mercedes usually had some spare time, and we would have a one-to-one mentoring session. This time though I brought all my paperwork with me so I could show Mercedes how I was getting on. Facebook page screenshots, website screenshots, etc. She advised me on changing the way some things were worded for the best possible impact. Though I was able to think up loads of ideas, I had trouble making them come out on paper in the right way. This is where she helped me the most.

Our mentoring sessions were held in some of London's most prestigious addresses. I was in Bank, London, one day, and everyone was walking around in beautifully fitting suits. Not one person had trainers or even jeans on. It was a completely different world to what I was used to. I was there though, in my suit, always trying to look the best I could. I do this little thing where I walk into the local supermarket and look at the champagne they have available. Normally you will see a bottle of Bollinger on the top shelf around £50-£60. But in Bank I remember walking in and bottles of Dom Perignon were on the shelves retailing at £250 a bottle! Bank was where the money is, excuse the pun.

It was around this time when I found out that not all people in suits are people to aspire to. When I was walking through the underground there was an old lady who was struggling with her bag, trying to get on the escalator. No one was helping her, so I walked over and assisted her with her bags, when someone said to his companion, "I will get to this meeting when this old granny and

If At First You Don't Succeed

bloke in a cheap suit get out of my way." My response to him was, quite frankly, unprintable, but he certainly got the message and walked off with a bright red face. I always remembered that moment, and I thought about buying a new suit. The money was starting to come in again and bills were starting to get paid off. So I didn't have to snatch all my money from the ATM every Friday when I got paid to stop creditors taking it all. Things were starting to take shape. When this business takes off, cheap suit no more. I will make sure I dress to match these posh twats and beat them all in business.

Back at work, I asked my boss to try and give me as many hours as he could. I wanted to put some money aside to get a nice place in London, to be with Laura, and also to be in a business environment. When I was in London I would feel a buzz that I can't explain, it was like I could smell money and success everywhere I went, and I wanted a piece of it.

By then I was working 90-110 hours a week, leaving very little time to be working on my business, but I still managed to squeeze in the odd hour here and there. Most of the time I was working on the sewers, digging down, sometimes with a digger, fixing the pipes and changing manhole covers in the roads. Clear-ups were the worst. That's where the sewage had come out over the top of a frame and cover, and spilled out all over someone's back garden, or even sometimes, into their house.

I would have to pick it all up, women's sanitary towels included, and put it into bags, which we nicknamed 'jam roly polys'.

I was still finding the time to work on my website whenever I could, and I finally got it finished after eight months hard work. I started to get jobs from other job search websites, with their permission, so I could get people who visited my site to apply for them. I would advertise them myself to get the applications. So, when I got my clients back, I would be ready to advertise their jobs properly.

This is when I thought about getting some help. I needed

someone to take my calls while I was working and just help with general administrative tasks. I advertised a job on PeoplePerHour and loads of people applied for it. I would just need someone a few hours a week. PeoplePerHour was perfect for this.

I met a woman called Amy; she was a single mother who had recently been laid off. She used to be a PA to a top executive in London, but due to child commitments she was having a lot of time off and they pretty much got rid of her.

Speaking with her on the phone I felt a feeling of similarity between my mum and Amy. Amy was keen, eager and wanted to help. I told her about my previous web designer who had screwed me over and that I was just starting again. She said, "I can do anything, I will even find everything there is to know about this man and send you over the information, just to show you how good I am." I could hear her children running around in the background and knew from my own experiences that the heart of a single mum is very determined, so I decided to give her a try.

True to her word, within 48 hours I had a plethora of information on the web designer. She had even found out he had put the job I had asked him to do on a similar website to PeoplePerHour, but based in India. He had asked someone in India to design the website for a fraction of the cost. Where the hell did the rest of the money go? The man was a fraud. I thanked her for finding this out, but by this time I was too into getting my business going again to worry about him anymore. That was in the past now, no point digging up the past, you're only going to get dirty. The only way to go is the future.

A Different World

A couple of months went by. Then I received an email from Danielle, who was now head of The Golden Touch and mentoring manager. I had been nominated for The Golden Touch Business Awards, in the 'Best idea for a business' and 'Young entrepreneur of the year' categories. Once I had picked myself up off the floor and pinched myself half a dozen times, in case it was some kind of cruel dream, it hit me as to what an achievement that was. The ceremony was to be held at a very luxurious hotel in London, but as sod's law would have it I was meant to be working that night and really needed the money. But this was an awards ceremony, how many times have I been nominated for an award? Never, is how many.

My boss was very supportive and swapped my shift so I could finish at 5pm. It would still be cutting it fine, but doable, and it would mean I still earned. Once my shift was over, I rushed home. I'd polished my shoes the night before but hadn't given a thought about what to wear. Should I go in a suit? Or wear my smart night-out clothes? It wasn't business as such, it was a party, so I opted to go with my smart going-out clothes. Jeans and a smart shirt.

The hotel was directly opposite the underground station, and my goodness, what a hotel it was. Without doubt the poshest hotel I had ever been to. Before this, the smartest hotel I had ever visited was a Travel Lodge on the motorway.

The hotel was indeed amazing. Marble everywhere, and glass cabinets full of incredibly high-priced gold and silver artwork. I walked up to the receptionist and asked where the Golden Touch Party was, and she asked me to wait as she phoned for a bellboy.

He arrived and announced that he was escorting me to the Sky bar. Wow, the Sky bar, just the sound of it sounded amazing. We stood in the lift and up it went, at a speed that I didn't realise lifts could travel.

The doors opened and I was immediately approached by a lady holding a silver tray full of glasses of champagne. She offered me a glass, which I found strange because it was free, but I was hardly going to say no to a glass of bubbly. It was an incredible setting, with white drapery and chandeliers everywhere. As I walked in and walked around, I immediately noticed I was one of just a few people there. After all that rushing I was early. The people that were already there were dressed incredibly smartly in tuxes, designer suits, cocktail dresses, etc. The waiters were also dressed impeccably and wore white gloves. I suddenly felt so out of place.

I stood in the corner of the room and tried to take it all in. I had never been to a party like this one. I noticed an open door and I stepped through to find a balcony that overlooked the entire city of London. The sun was just setting and it looked quite beautiful. I stood there with my glass of bubbly and tried to enjoy the moment. I then heard the door open and close, and a gentleman came out and said, "You look very lonely out here."

We started chatting and I soon found out that he was another Golden Touch mentor. He was used to this type of event and urged me to come back inside. I walked in and he introduced me to a few other people who had just shown up, who were again dressed in suits. I then began going from person to person, introducing myself, passing out business cards and hearing people introduce themselves. It felt amazing to be in with the right crowd, this was the exact place I wanted to be and who I wanted to be with.

Waiting staff walked around with silver trays with full glasses of drink on them; it was all paid for and you could have as much as you wanted.

I went back outside on the balcony to see the daylight slowly slip away beyond the buildings. Now feeling slightly drunk, I looked down at the champagne in my hand and couldn't help but smile. Nearly there, I am nearly there.

Then it was the big moment, time for the awards. Everyone gathered around, and Jason, who was the MD of Golden Touch, stood up to present the awards. Jason was wearing jeans and a nice shirt too, he was still his flamboyant self, always standing out from the crowd. Soon, the first award I was nominated for came up. 'Best idea for a business'. A big drum roll, and then... No, it wasn't me. Then soon after, the next award that I was up for, the big one for the night, 'Young entrepreneur of the year'. Another big drum roll... No, it wasn't me again. My new friend Gary, another mentee, had won that one. He had an extremely good idea for a business and was doing very well with it, so I was glad he got it. Even though I was a tiny bit envious, it couldn't have gone to a nicer and more deserving man.

I walked around congratulating all the winners. I was by now half drunk and really enjoying myself. I then went back out onto the balcony and enjoyed a final look at the amazing bird's eye view of nighttime London. I started feeling like everything was beginning to look up in my life, and it could only get better. I didn't win any of the awards, but it wasn't my time just yet. It was coming, but not yet.

The award party finished and everyone started to leave. I thanked Jason for a quality night, and he told me the party was still going on. He and a few others were heading for a few drinks at a club where he was a member, and would I like to join them? Hell yeah! We all jumped in the lift, walked back through the lobby and waited for a few more people, then headed to Jason's members' club which was a short walk down the road.

Walking in, it looked a bit like an office at first. We were greeted by a receptionist, Jason signed us all in, and we walked to the lift. When we got to the top, the doors opened and we walked around to the right and into a very elegant bar.

It was plain to see that there were a lot of well-to-do people there. Aadi told me there was a former Premier League manager sitting in the corner. Don't ask me who it was, I was pretty drunk at

The Dreamer

the time, but Aadi introduced me and I shook his hand.

I handed out a few more business cards to people I was meeting, just remembering to be full of confidence in my business. "We are going to take the UK by storm, look at the backers we have. This is going to be something extremely successful and this business I have created will put a lot of young people back into work."

I walked back to the bar and got a cocktail. I looked around and realised all that worrying was for nothing. I could fit in, I could become one of them. Even though at the time I wasn't wearing a suit, I still felt like I was one of the suits. It's not a flashy suit or an expensive watch that makes you a good businessman, it's your heart. If you want something that much and are prepared to go through hell to get it, you will be rewarded with something worth more than money. You will gain confidence, pride and self-respect. No matter how much money you have, you can't buy that. Once you have that inside you and it's burning away, no one can touch you.

I got home in the early hours of the morning after catching the last train from Victoria. Though still in my dingy flat, I felt great that I was getting somewhere. The picture of my dream house was still on the wall, still with the power to drive me and my business forward. I would go to work, shovel shit, but at the same time would have people doing sales calls for me. I'd then advertise the jobs. Soon I had a few regular clients, and it was starting to all come together.

It was getting close to Christmas again. My boss called me and asked if I could come and see him one night after work. It was then that he explained that he was struggling to find me work and could only offer me two or three days a week.

That wasn't enough for me, and I'd been thinking for a while about taking the big leap and working on my business full-time.

I told my boss I was very grateful to him, but it was time to go it alone and give it my best to make Next Generation Jobs a success.

Moment Of Truth

I left that flat in Cliftonville. I remember the excitement as I started to pack up the things I would take to London and threw away the stuff I no longer needed. Then I went back for one last look around the place, thinking about when I moved in, the wind blowing through the closed window and the Christmas I'd spent with Laura on the mattress on the floor, eating our turkey sandwiches. I was finally getting out. I was moving forward!

I had saved some money over the months and decided to go where the money was. London. It's the place where I could make my business a success and make my dreams come true. I found a lovely little place by a canal on the outskirts of London. It was a fresh start for me and Laura; we had become somewhat distant over the past few months. I could spend more time with her and work on my business full time.

I used all the savings I had to get us up there, we had enough for three months' rent. I'd put myself in a position where it was make or break for my company. I knew it would be a success and I could make money from it, I just had to devote my life to it. The timing was perfect. January is the busiest time of the year for recruitment, so I set that month for the official launch of Next Generation Jobs.

Though it was already up and running, having an official launch meant that I could send out marketing materials to companies and the press. I was stepping it up a gear now. I began to put all the right plans into place to make sure I had a good first month. I applied for second-stage funding from the banks but was denied. They didn't even look at my business plan or care about how much money I could make from the business. Just gave me a flat no. I hadn't planned for that. I thought because I could prove I was doing well and needed a bit more funding to catapult Next Generation Jobs to the next level, it would be a given. I had all the plans and structure in place, as well as strong economic figures. It was just so frustrating that they wouldn't look at any of it. I was starting to fear I had made a huge mistake in risking everything I had on this move.

Despite now living in an amazing house in a quality location, I was in a predicament, as I needed more funds so I could launch the company properly. Fortune was smiling on me though, and a very dear friend of mine came to the rescue and loaned me £1,000. It wasn't the £10,000 I had asked Second Stage Start-up for, but it was something that I could work with.

I rewrote all my plans and preparations for launching with £1,000, rather than £10,000. I found all the best deals I could. I got all the preparations in place and while everyone else was playing Christmas party games, drinking wine and wearing festive hats, I was working every hour of every day, running a trial week to see how many applications I could get for the jobs on my website. And I was right, my plans were perfect. I got five hundred applications in a trial week over Christmas, just using some local companies that needed temp staff over the Christmas holidays. I had found a gap in the market and was now able to exploit it.

I briefed Amy and said, "This is it, 2014 will now be the start of something very special. Let's really go for it this year and make this business a success. I'm going to rely on you a hell of a lot." She just laughed and said, "I'm ready for anything, you know me." She was absolutely fantastic to have in my corner.

Over the Christmas period I was working around twenty hours a day getting the last bits sorted for the launch. Amy then called me and said she had found a company that could populate my website with jobs. This company would pay me per application from my website.

What a fantastic find. I just needed to code in the XML feed into job postings. This made it look like I had a hell of a lot more jobs on Next Generation Jobs. The companies I was advertising for were also placed into the list so there were some of mine and this company's jobs. The company paid £0.10 to £0.60 per application.

I coded the XML feed to place the jobs I wanted, all entry level so it suited the website. The job categories on the website started to fill up and after a few days there were thousands of jobs listed on the website.

I was finally ready for the big launch. I already had a press release written up and had it scheduled for release on the day after New Year. It was sent to absolutely everyone I could think of. I had unlimited minutes on my phone and I made the most of it, calling everyone relevant, to tell them Next Generation Jobs was here and was the place to go for young people to find work.

I was doing everything in my power to make this business a success; I would get up at 4am and work right through the day until 2am. So focused was I on my goals, I would forget to eat and drink sometimes, wanting to achieve the ultimate success. I would literally be living on my laptop, sometimes falling asleep at it for a couple of hours, and as soon as I woke up, refreshing my emails to see if I had any new ones.

We had set up a room in the house as a little makeshift office. I closed the door and just went for it. I never saw much of Laura; she was working a lot and when she was home I was always working.

Applications started flying in. I had a call from Amy telling me I had made an absolute fortune already with the XML feed we had incorporated on the website. It had only been available for a few days and already hundreds of people were applying every day.

All this hard work was starting to pay off. After a week, I received an email from my local newspaper which wanted to come and interview me and take some pictures. This was the start, the business was absolutely flying over the space of the first week, and I had applications pouring in for all my jobs.

The newspaper was for Kent, the area where I was from, so I had to travel back to Margate train station to meet them. On the train, I revised the public relations notes I'd taken from my mentoring with Mercedes. I also emailed Mercedes, and within the hour she had called me to prep me over the phone for the interview. It was a shot of confidence again, just what I needed, as I was heading into the unknown.

As I continued my journey, I pondered the irony of it all. I was now going *to* Margate, rather than leaving it to go up to London. I also found it quite empowering that a reporter wanted to interview me, and feature me in their paper. Finally, all this hard work was getting me somewhere. I began to realise that it was all about confidence. Once you have confidence in yourself you can do anything you want and get anywhere you want. But you can't be too confident otherwise you will come across as cocky, and nobody likes someone that's cocky. It's a very fine line, and you need to always be aware of that.

I was now speaking with my parents again. We'd made up and were now over our little tiff. My mum had thankfully fully recovered. I had asked the photographer to meet me at my parents' house for the pictures. Just before I pulled into Margate, I had another phone call, from another local newspaper. They also wanted an interview with me. This was starting to become unreal.

I told them I was in Margate for that day and if they could meet me at my parents' place, I would be there all day. Two newspaper interviews in one day, I felt like Alan Sugar. But it didn't end there.

After my press interviews, I received another call.

"Hi, this is the news desk at the BBC. Am I speaking with David Brett?"

I nearly fell off my chair. I now had the BBC coming around the following day to do an interview. That night I went up to Tesco to get a nice bottle of Prosecco. I still didn't have any money yet, but it was soon to be coming my way. Strange how life turns out. This time last year I was in the same store, but looking for the cheapest thing I could find, just to have something to eat.

My parents let me stay at their house for the night, but I couldn't sleep. It felt like a wonderful dream, one that I never wanted to wake from. I lay there, looking at the ceiling, wondering where I would be in another year's time. Maybe I could be living in my own house, that house I always wanted, that was fully paid for. I imagined lying in my own bed, looking at the ceiling, knowing it was *my* ceiling, that I could paint the walls any colour I wanted, knowing no one had any control over me in *my* house.

The next day I woke up very early, probably because I was used to waking up at 4am. I just kept going over what I was going to say, while I made sure my suit was pristine. I stood there, ironing it for what seemed like hours, getting Sellotape and trying to get any hairs or specks of dust off it. As I stood in front of the mirror, trying to take it all in, I felt as though I was on a roller coaster, and all I could do was enjoy the ride. So that's exactly what I did, I just went with it and enjoyed everything that came at me.

I phoned Jason and told him what was happening, he was so happy for me. I also phoned Mercedes and she gave me another of her pep talks. Seriously, she could convince an Eskimo to go and do his fishing in his underpants. But she also reminded me not to neglect my business whilst doing all this press and to keep my feet on the ground, as there was still a lot of hard work ahead. After the call, I stood in front of the mirror again, this time practicing what I would say.

I walked up and down the hallway in my parents' house, eagerly awaiting the arrival of the BBC. THE BBC! I still couldn't believe it. Through the front door window I saw a car pull up, and I immediately recognised the man who climbed out. It was one of the main presenters of the news show. He began walking towards my house. I walked back into the front room, looked one more time into the mirror, making sure I looked like how a successful entrepreneur should. I didn't know if I should open the door to welcome him or wait in the front room and pretend I hadn't seen him. So I played it cool and just kept looking in the mirror.

The doorbell rang, I opened the door and shook his hand. He walked in and sat across from me, on the sofa. He had a huge black bag with him, and after we spoke briefly, he unzipped it and took out a camera. We decided that the conservatory was the best place to carry out the interview, so we went in, and he began connecting me up with a microphone - fitting a battery pack to my belt, then attaching the microphone to my tie. I had always seen people on TV with one of those little microphones on their ties but had never thought I would ever have one on. It was a bizarre experience. I then sat there, eagerly waiting for him to set up the camera. I was overwhelmed by everything that was happening. I don't think it looked like it though, as I had a massive grin on my face.

Everything now set up, he sat in front of me, and that was it - my legs and hands started to tremble.

He began asking his questions. I was on autopilot as I had practiced most of them before he arrived. In the back of my mind I was just thinking, "How the hell did I get here? I'm being interviewed on the BBC, ME, just because I started my own business, started from scribbling on a piece of paper in my work van."

I had prepared for this most of the morning, but nothing can really prepare you for when the time actually comes. We spoke about where I had come from to where I was now. I told him the flat I used to live in was just up the road if he wanted to go see it. He did, so I jumped in his car and we drove the short ride to my old flat in Cliftonville.

I got out and the feeling of being back at where it all began was incredible. This is where my dream began, my little adventure. Now I'm back here with a BBC presenter; who would have thought it? He began filming me walking up the road, looking up at my old flat and walking off in the distance. You have no idea how good that felt to me.

Moment Of Truth

It was only a few weeks earlier I had left, but it felt like a lifetime ago.

He dropped me back at my parents' house and I shook his hand as he wished me all the best, telling me that I had a very bright future ahead of me. I walked back into the house and sat down, trying to go over what had just happened over the past couple of days.

It was starting to get late now. I felt I had to go out for a walk, and decided to go back to my old flat again. This time I was dressed in a suit and had more than £20 in the bank. I walked down the dark and eerie road where my flat was. The pride that came over me was unreal. I knew I could get out of there, I knew I would do it. I walked up to just outside and looked up again. No one was in my old flat, and I couldn't see the light on. I just stood there reminiscing over lying on a mattress on the floor with a few blankets.

I got up early the next morning and began traveling back up to London. My phone rang. It was the local Kent radio station, requesting an interview. It really was getting crazy. It was like I was being pulled in loads of directions. I agreed to the interview and got off at one of the stations on my route back to London and met with a lady who recorded me on her phone. That was later played over and over again on the radio station's news.

It was so hard to try and keep on top of everything while still meeting with everyone. That week I had been in two newspapers and on the radio and the BBC news. Some people work their whole lives on a business and don't get that kind of press, and I'd got all that in the first official month of my business. I went online and typed in my name to see what would happen. I was top of the page; my business was right next to pictures of me with the story. I was featured in other online news feeds I didn't even know about. I was literally everywhere. Next Generation Jobs was taking off.

Amy was in overdrive. She was getting requests for meetings for me and jobs continued to pour in. The website was still only partially the dream I wanted it to be. It was only listing jobs. But that was

The Dreamer

hard enough to keep on top of by itself. Step by step and I will create the dream website.

Living the Dream

When I was finally back in my place in London, I began trying to capitalise on all the attention I had received. My phone hadn't stopped ringing. Everyone seemed to want to talk to me. Trying to recover from all of this madness, I got a call from Daybreak, asking if I would be available to come in and sit on their sofa live on the TV. I thought it was a prank from one of my old workmates; local radio and TV is one thing, but Daybreak had over two million viewers. But alas, it never happened, as a big story hit the news and they had to allocate the slot to that. Of course, I was disappointed but took the positives from it. It was such a privilege just to be asked to come in. Then I had an afterthought. Disappointed not to talk in front of two million people? It wasn't too long ago when I was shitting myself over the prospect of talking to a hundred.

Soon after, I got a call from Jason. He told me about an event he would be holding in a few months. It was another start-up loans meeting for new Golden Touch mentees. But this one was going to be huge. Sir Bob Geldof was going to be there, giving a motivational speech. Bob Geldof, the man behind Live Aid, which raised over a hundred and fifty million pounds to fight famine in Ethiopia and other African countries, and who persuaded some of the biggest pop and rock artists in the world to perform for free.

Gone were the days of the shy bloke who believed everyone when they called him a hopeless dreamer. I was now a confident, highly motivated and successful business owner. But in Bob's league? I don't think so. I've never had a number-one record in the charts for a start. Not yet, anyway.

Whilst everything with the business was booming, my relationship with my Laura started to deteriorate. I was so excited about everything going on but she just didn't seem to care. I would

The Dreamer

be jumping around the room each time I reached another success, wanting to share it with her, to celebrate together, talk to her about all the amazing things that were happening, but she just didn't want to hear. At one point, after receiving some great news about the business, I was afraid to tell her in case it ended in another argument.

Things then slowly got worse. I made more effort to keep things going. I would try to get her attention in various ways, such as doing extra things around the house, making her breakfasts in bed, making sure dinner was ready for when she got home from work, and that it was food that she loved. But nothing changed, she barely noticed the efforts I was making. We then began not talking to each other and she would always be on the phone either texting or talking to someone. I began to think I wasn't what she wanted anymore and maybe someone else had her attention.

I carried on with what I was doing and kept working all the hours I could from home, combined with going to meetings in London with clients to pick up more business. I was absolutely flying in my professional life, I loved that part of it, and felt that I was invincible.

I started to prepare myself for the Golden Touch event. I would stand in the front room, practicing my speech, over and over, to make sure it was absolutely perfect.

Cheap suit? I remember the remark from the bloke on the underground. The money was now rolling in. Each month the businesses we displayed jobs for would send us payment for the applications received via our website. We were also making money from job postings that Amy had set up or from the telesales people whom Amy had hired to call businesses.

In that first month (January 2014) we had received nearly 35,000 applications from young people looking for work and were looking to keep this going into the next month.

But this event was coming up for the Golden Touch and I wanted to look the part. I phoned Amy and said, "Amy, where can I get a suit? I'm not talking any suit. I want to look like Mark Darcy from

Bridget Jones's Diary." She said she used to know a shop in Savile Row that did suits at excellent prices for the area and I'd look like a real managing director. "Can you call them and arrange a fitting?" I said back. She replied, "Yes, no problem, I think the owner is still there. I'll see if I can work some charm and magic."

True to her word, within a few days I had a fitting at a very prestigious tailoring company in Savile Row. I wanted to portray the image of a successful businessman; one of those people I'd idolised on the trips to London when I was starting out. So I ended up spending around £5,000 on a new suit. This included a raincoat and leather gloves. Mark Darcy, eat your heart out.

I practiced in the mirror trying to hone my skills for public speaking. My accent was still very common, so I tried to make sure I pronounced my words correctly to sound a bit posher, like a real businessman.

While I was on the phone to Amy one day, she mentioned that Regus was doing a promotion for office space and had got in touch, offering a free trial. Regus have offices all over the UK and offer office space or just a prestigious address so businesses can register themselves there. I said, "What sort of offices are they offering then?" She replied, "I don't know, a representative just phoned to ask if we would be interested." I said, "Work your magic Amy, see if you can get us an office address in Canary Wharf, that's where the big businesses are."

She phoned back within a few hours. "You've got it. Next Generation Jobs now has a business address on the 37th floor of 1 Canada Square, Canary Wharf. They asked if you would like to come down and see it?" Hell yeah, I wanted to come and see it!

It wasn't an office I was going to be working in, but just an address for the business. It was a nice touch and it was free for three months!

I got my expensive suit on and caught the train to Canary Wharf, definitely feeling I was starting to fit in now. I remember coming out in an underground station that was full of shops. In the distance I saw three chairs high up against the wall. A gentleman was sitting there reading a newspaper. When I got closer I saw he was getting his shoes polished.

I stood looking, then glanced at my shoes. Before I even had a chance to think about it a man turned to me and said, "Would Sir like to have his shoes polished?" Sir would bloody definitely like his shoes polished, I thought! But I replied in a posher voice, "Oh yes, why not." So I sat down and was handed the Financial Times. The paper was huge and the guy started polishing my pretty much brand new shoes I'd just bought.

I had no idea what I was reading in the paper, it was all about financial markets. So I just concentrated on the news sections.

After a while, "Is Sir happy with the shoes?" "Yes, they are fantastic!" He had made them incredibly shiny. They somehow looked even newer than when I bought them. I handed over £30 to him and carried on walking towards 1 Canada Square. Walking outside I just had to see this building up close, it's the biggest building in Canary Wharf and right next to HSBC London Headquarters.

You can definitely tell it, too. I stood next to it and peered into the sky. It looked like it never ended. Because it's so tall, at night there is a pulsating light flashing at the top to ward off unsuspecting aircraft.

Time to go in. As you walk in there's marble absolutely everywhere. This is obviously a sign of wealth I thought, as I remembered seeing this at the posh hotel I went to for the awards. The main reception was a huge white desk with ONE CANADA SQUARE written on it. Behind the desk was a brownish/red marble that covered the wall to the ceiling. Fresh flowers stood at the side of the reception desk. I walked over and was asked for my name and business. "David Brett Managing Director of Next Generation Jobs. I have just acquired an office on the 37th floor and have come to see it."

The receptionist then asked me to wait while she phoned that floor. I was then given a pass and shown towards the automated door, where you had to show your pass to get in.

I pressed for the lift and waited to get in, then clicked the 37th floor. The doors opened and at the end of the corridor was another desk, this one inlaid with beautiful wooden patterns. Before I had a chance to even get to the desk a lady came straight up to me and said, "Mr Brett?" She then showed me around the floor and the office space I could use for a fee if needed in the future. "Maybe your staff could use this space, it has a beautiful view and we could let it out to you for a very good rate." I said, "Well maybe this space could be good for the future, but at the moment I am just a one-man band with Amy as my PA." She then showed me a meeting room, in a central position of the floor. Glass completely surrounded the room, but it was hazed so no one could see in. An oval table dominated the room. "This room can be hired out for your clients; we can also provide refreshments and coffee."

I asked, "Could I just take one more look at the office space and call my PA?" I wasn't going to rent it, I just wanted to have a look at the room by myself. The let was incredibly expensive and I didn't have any staff to fill it with anyway. But what a view. The office was fully furnished, and I walked around just imagining me having people working at these desks, all working for Next Generation Jobs. I decided to sit down, put my feet up on the desk and take a picture of it all, the view included.

I left there and never went back again. This was something for the future, but not yet. The address and use of the meeting room would be good enough for me for now.

For the moment I just had to concentrate on keeping the business going, keeping the money rolling in and most importantly trying to get young people back to work.

Then the day finally came when I had to speak for The Golden

The Dreamer

Touch at the event. Out came my very expensive suit again, cheap suit no more! I caught the underground into central London and met with other Golden Touch mentees under the clock at London Waterloo station. I knew a few of them, but everyone seemed to know me.

They came up to me, showing me their ideas and asking me what I thought of them. I was quite flattered.

We left the train station and began the short walk to the event. My stomach was, as usual, in knots. It helped my confidence, for some reason. I began to look down at my clothes, my shoes still gleaming from being polished. I was making it.

The event was in an office building, and we had the basement. I walked downstairs and straight away bumped into Mercedes. She asked me how I was feeling, and I said that I was a little nervous, but was confident that I could pull it off. She explained that she wasn't invited to the event but heard that I would be speaking, so came down specially to support me. Again, I felt flattered.

We discussed the things I would be saying. I had ten to fifteen minutes to speak in front of everyone. Mercedes started giving me some words of confidence, a bit like a trainer would do to a boxer who was just about to get in the ring. Telling me I was going to smash it, people are going to love me, that once I was up there, people were going to be very envious.

The sound man for the event then approached me and fitted me with a microphone, the same kind that I'd used for my BBC interview. As he was attaching the battery pack Mercedes asked me if I was ready.

I was still in disbelief about where I was and how the hell I got here, but yes, I was ready. We walked in and the room was full of young entrepreneurs looking for a start in business, about 250 people overall. Mercedes and I went in and sat in the front row, and then it was the big introduction. Jason, MD of Golden Touch mentoring, came on stage. He gave a big and amazing introduction to the

Golden Touch Youth project.

I was then introduced, and everyone applauded. I got up out of my seat and Mercedes stood up with me. I looked around the room and could see all those eyes on me.

We climbed onto the stage, Mercedes standing alongside me, like every good corner man (or woman in this case), and I started my rehearsed speech, using my new-found technique of looking just above the tops of people's heads. I was a little worried that the nerves were getting the better of me, so it wasn't until I was about five minutes in that I started looking around the room, glancing at one person, then at the next. Soon, I started looking at people in the eyes, and as I relaxed a little I could feel that I was connecting with the audience. I had never been able to do this before, and oddly, soon started to enjoy it. I could see people's facial expression change as I went through the story of my business journey. When I was talking about my flat and living on £2 a day it was one of sorrow, then as I started to near the end and talking about the press and all the success I was having, it turned to happiness and excitement.

Before I knew it, my speech was over. I received a huge round of applause which seemed to go on for ages. Mercedes then took the stage and asked if there were any questions they had for me, and there was one I particularly remember. Someone asked how I did it. My answer was simple. I never gave up. Even when it gets tough and you just want to quit, take it slow, just put one foot in front of the other, and keep plugging away.

We walked off to another big round of applause, and Mercedes told me that she was very proud of me. The sound guy came around to the front and asked me to come with him while he took off the microphone. As he did, he said what an amazing speech it was.

Receiving flattering comments seemed to be the common theme of the evening. I was pleased with myself though. I had struggled to speak to a crowd of fewer than twenty people not too long ago, and now I'd just finished addressing a room of about two hundred and fifty, talking for fifteen minutes. It was a real milestone in my life.

I walked back into the room, and Sir Bob Geldof had turned up. I sat down next to Mercedes and listened as he spoke of how he started up his company, and how he was told by a bank that they wouldn't help fund it, so he found funding elsewhere and started up a newspaper that became extremely successful.

It just goes to show that everyone in life has knockbacks, it's just how you respond to them. You can either look at other avenues or you can quit. They always say that 99% of the people who quit their dreams work for the 1% who didn't give up.

As Sir Bob finished, there was a little break. Everyone was moving around, and people were trying to come up to me to talk to me, but Mercedes wanted me to have a picture with Sir Bob. He had gone upstairs to have pictures taken for the national paper. We followed him. There were cameras everywhere, snapping away at Sir Bob and Jason, then Jason waved me over to come into the picture. As I walked over, Mercedes began checking my tie and brushing off my jacket. I felt great, like the true businessman I'd always wanted to be.

As I stood with them, Sir Bob made a cheeky remark about how he hoped I hadn't started up my own hair salon. It was an obvious dig about my hairstyle. Bit rich coming from him, and I thought, "Does this guy own a mirror?!"

After all the pictures with the press, I had a quick chat with Sir Bob, and he commented on how he thought my business was a brilliant idea and wished me luck for the future. I instantly forgave him for his jibe about my hairstyle.

The rest of the event was quite formal and at the end I had a line of people waiting to speak with me, seeking advice. Again, I found it a little strange, as it wasn't too long ago when it was me asking all the questions. Life, you can't predict it. I really didn't mind how long it took, I just wanted to help as many people as I could to start their own dream with some tips I had learnt.

When it came to an end, I headed for the pub along with the Golden Touch team. Mercedes got a round in and we all chatted about the evening. Aadi mentioned that some people were asking about me when I was having my picture taken with Sir Bob. Again, reality check, having my picture taken with Sir Bob Geldof. Yep, that happened. Amazing!

When I got home, I told Laura that I'd had a blinding day and that I wanted to treat her. I took her to a lovely restaurant where I'd heard the food was excellent and indeed it was. I even splashed out on some of the champagne. But even that didn't change the way she looked upon me, it was as though she had become disinterested. It may have been because I was spending a lot of time working and not enough time on our relationship, or that she had simply gone off me. Whichever it was, it hurt. Particularly as she refused to discuss why she was acting as she was. I loved her more than anything. I leaned on her so much for strength during my down times. She was also my best friend.

Striving For Success Against All The Odds

I decided it was best not to let it affect me too much, so threw myself into work even more, thinking if I bought a house and gave her half, everything would all be okay again. There was no way I could get a mortgage with my credit rating, so the only way to buy one was outright. I called companies, getting more and more jobs posted online. I gathered as many job seekers as I could, and the applications kept flying in. I was feeling so confident in myself. I phoned one business, and the guy mocked me saying, "You are just a tiny little company, how are you going to get me quality applications?"

If that had happened a few months earlier I would have been tongue-tied and let him off the hook. But this was a new me. I said, "I tell you what - you post one job online and I will guarantee you at least fifty applications." He agreed, and I advertised the absolute hell out of the job, posting it every single place I could. I ended up getting over two hundred applications in only a few days. It ended up having so many applications that he had to pull it off the website. He then became a repeat customer.

Money was rolling in each month and Amy was pretty much working as many hours as she could to keep up with the admin.

I phoned Jason one day and asked him if he was available for a chat. I had been wanting to meet with him for ages, and it seemed that the time was right to have a sit-down and pick his brain.

He said he would pick me up from the station as he was driving into London from Richmond that day. So, I got the underground into central London and stood outside waiting.

I heard a huge roar coming down the street, it was the sound of a very nice sports car. Then it came around the corner and you could see it was a Maserati, it sounded like a tiger roaring. Then it pulled up in front of me, Jason wound down the window and said, "Morning Dave, jump in mate." I had never been in a supercar before, this must have cost at least £100k. We drove down the streets of London and chatted about the monster of a car. Jason told me it did nineteen miles to the gallon… WOW.

We then pulled up at a very posh restaurant somewhere in Mayfair. We got out and Jason gave his key, which was the size of a brick, to the doorman who drove the car away to park it. "Reservation for Jason of Golden Touch," he said to the lady greeting us. She said, "Oh yes, Sir, we have your usual spot next to the window."

We sat down and were given menus. I kept looking at mine and thinking I didn't like half this stuff on here, it's all salmon, scallops, roasted marrowbone… and spiced pigeon. That made me laugh, I wondered if they'd picked one up off the streets, there is an abundance! But nothing on the menu was to my liking. Then I noticed there were no prices shown.

Jason then said while looking at the wine list, "You can have anything you want on me, in celebration of your success." I thought that was such a nice gesture, but what to have? I asked Jason, "Do they do steaks here?" He then called over the waitress. "Dave wants to know if you have any steaks, he wants one, can you do it?"

She replied, "Yes, I'm sure we can." Within a few minutes she returned, saying, "We have a lovely filet mignon, Sir." I ordered that and Jason had the same. When it came out I was so used to a nice pub lunch at 'Spoons, I didn't realise it didn't come with chips. Just a steak on its own on the plate. I asked Jason, "Where's the chips?" He called the waitress back over. "Dave wants some chips too. You want anything else Dave?" Someone then came over and gave Jason some broccoli that looked delicious. I asked for some of that too.

We then chatted over dinner about how my business was doing and he asked me what the next stage was. I hadn't really thought about that. He suggested going for some big investment, but only if I

The Dreamer

was comfortable with the idea. He said, "You can grow your business organically or look for outside investment; we're talking maybe along the lines of six figures if your business has the revenue streams you are telling me. Have a think, I don't mind being a second mentor to you alongside Mercedes. I don't want any fees. I just love your story and would like to be a part of it."

We finished our discussion and went our separate ways. I kept thinking all the way home, "What is the next step?" To be honest I hadn't even planned on getting this far. What would the next step be?

I was in my office at home and had YouTube on in the background, it flicked through different songs. Then 'The Apprentice' song came up. That got me thinking. People go on The Apprentice to go halves on a business venture with Lord Sugar! And you get £250k investment.

I felt at that time that I could do any role in any company, it was a fantastic feeling, like I could conquer the whole world. I saw The Apprentice was taking auditions in the next few weeks. Coincidence? I decided to pluck up the courage and apply. Soon after applying I was sent an email to attend an audition in central London. I got down to the final interview stages, but decided it wasn't really for me. I didn't want to be a 'former' Apprentice contestant or 'The Apprentice winner'. I wanted to be me. I wanted to be the guy from the streets who made it on his own.

I wish I could tell you more about The Apprentice, but I had to tick a box on my application to say that I am not allowed to talk about the audition process, which is a shame because there are so many secrets I would like to tell. I will say this though - the rude woman who told me, "Is that all you have done?" got a right earful before I walked out.

It was another experience to add to the belt, all clouds have a silver lining.

When I was searching for applicants for a few jobs on other websites, I noticed on one guy's CV that he was a professional body language expert. I phoned him to have a chat, and he told me that he used to be a professional poker player and had come over from the USA to try and get a job as a professional interviewer.

I asked for a meeting and said I would pay him to teach me a few things. We met in a café in London and he started telling me some amazing stuff. He told me about eye movements when asking questions. He taught me it's not the questions you ask and the answers you receive, it's more to do with the body language you present when answering the questions. Like shifting your body weight when asked an awkward question, and that wearing a watch is supposed to show a sign of good timekeeping.

I wrote it all down and became fascinated by it. I met with him a few more times after that. I felt it was an essential part of recruitment. I would spend some of my spare time researching more and more.

I was then contacted by a lady who had heard me talk at the Golden Touch event, and she asked me if I could meet with her. When we did she told me about her business, which sounded like a great idea. Then she whipped out a pen and paper and started writing down ideas I was coming up with, she called it 'picking my brain'. I didn't think anything I was saying was particularly great, but whenever I suggested something she smiled and scribbled it down.

I told Mercedes about this and she said, "People are trying to get you to help their business. If you have the time you can do it for free. But if not, you can start charging people for a one-to-one session." One-to-one session with *me*? Just for my ideas? I didn't think they were that great, but I always had a knack for coming up with inventions. When I was very young I drew up and showed my stepdad a way to heat a room using hot water in a metal container. Being very young I didn't know this was how central heating worked, but I had designed it.

Before starting Next Generation Jobs I really wanted to build a self-running bathtub. You could turn it on from your phone and it

The Dreamer

would fill up to the desired temperature and depth, with bubbles, waiting for you when you got home, then start beeping at you if you forgot to get in, like your washing machine does when it's finished a cycle. I loved this idea, but it was just far too complex to get moving at that time.

A few weeks later Amy sent me a link to another competition called 'The Recruitment Entrepreneur'. It was a James Caan venture, where he invests £500,000 into your recruitment idea and provides you with his personal mentoring. I remember thinking to myself that this was made for me, it seemed perfect. You may recall that James Caan was the ex-Dragons' Den investor whom I saw at Olympia when I first came up with the idea for Next Generation Jobs. His words were, "If you have a business idea, believe in it, believe in yourself, go to the person you are showing it to and have passion. Say, 'I have a fantastic business idea, what do you think?'"

That started me off on my business venture and now I had a chance to be his Recruitment Entrepreneur. I was filling out my application when I came across a section headed 'Recruitment Experience'. I was in a bit of a dilemma. If I could explain to him face to face what I had done, rather than my past experience, I'd have been home and dry, but on paper, when asked that simple question, I looked very inexperienced. So for 'How many years experience', I had to put a big fat zero as the answer. I wasn't satisfied with that, this was a lifetime opportunity and a life-changing potential investment, so I decided to write an accompanying letter to try and increase my chances of getting selected.

I tried my absolute best to sell myself and the company. I put that Next Generation Jobs is the 'go to' place for young people to find entry-level jobs. I also wrote that I only launched properly at the start of the year and had already achieved a huge success, and although working the business on my own, I had managed to receive nearly 30,000 applications in the first month alone. I added that Next Generation Jobs now had a social media following of around fifty thousand and was getting around two thousand five hundred people visiting the website every day, looking for jobs and posting new jobs. I had achieved all this on my own, working from home, with very little startup funding.

I finished off my application, then imagined what I could do with a half a million pounds investment. The company that was handling it all were called Hamilton and Bradshaw, so I found out where the office was in Mayfair and personally posted the letter through their door. I thought if I didn't get through the application stage, at least I had done everything I possibly could, so could walk away with my head held high.

A few days later I was sent an email from Hamilton and Bradshaw. My application had been successful. I was asked to attend a meeting at their offices, but this wasn't for a month or two. I thought to myself, right, now is the time to sort out the weakness in my application. When I go for this meeting they will try and pick holes in the bad aspects, so I have to show I will do whatever it takes. I didn't want to sit there in the meeting for them to ask what job I did before and I say, "I worked on the sewers mopping up people's shit." I needed to be tactical and think ahead about what they would pick up, so I went online that day and applied for over one hundred recruitment consultant positions all around London. I didn't tell them about my business, they could only see I had literally come from working in the sewers and was now trying to get a job in recruitment.

It was hard to sell myself because it's a completely different industry. But I was persistent.

The day after I sent all the applications I called every single one of them, asking to speak with the person recruiting the position I had applied for. Once through, I would ask what they thought about my CV, and even if they said I wasn't suitable for the role that I had applied for, I would push them into giving me feedback. It's always good to ask. Then one company asked me to come for an interview the very next day. They told me they would be sending a welcome pack over for me to have a look at, so that I could get to know the company and what they do.

I told myself, "This job is mine." I visualised it all happening, shaking the hands of the interviewer as they told me I was in. If you believe in what you want, there is a far higher likelihood of it happening. Like a teenager going for a driving test. If he thinks he's going to fail, he probably will, but if he thinks he's going to pass, he will be more confident and stand a much better chance.

That night I didn't work on my business. Instead, I devoted all my time to learning about this new company that I would be working for and revising my notes from the meetings I'd had with the body language expert. I learned about when the business first started, where it first started, the director of the business, the different roles within the company, the sectors they worked in, everything that was available.

The next day as I walked to the building where I would be having my interview, a friend sent me a text saying that if I didn't concentrate on my business full time, I'd be throwing it all away. The thing is, with me, I like to keep my cards close to my chest and play them at the end when no one is expecting it.

This job, when I got it, was only a stepping stone for me and would support my application for when I would attend the Recruitment Entrepreneur meeting in a few months' time. I'd tell them what I had achieved at this recruitment company in only a few months, just to prove that Next Generation Jobs, my business, wasn't a fluke and I was the real deal.

With that in mind I walked into the building and made sure people would remember me. I shook everyone's hand as I introduced myself, made them laugh, and demonstrated my glowing confidence. I'd also put on my sharpest suit. Then I sat down and the interview started. Game on, I thought. I started using all the techniques I'd been taught; small details are the key. I was sailing through the interview. We small-talked for a while, and exchanged a few niceties, then came out the trump card, "What do you know about the company?"

Bingo. Big smile and a deep breath. I started listing their offices throughout the world, the sectors they worked in, and was halfway through describing when the company first started when I was asked to stop. I wasn't sure if I had done something wrong, but I could still see the interviewer's body language was positive towards me. I was right, as he then proceeded to thank me for taking the initiative to learn about the company, it showed I was serious by taking the time to research.

We small-talked a bit more and he then asked why I wanted to swap from working on the roads to sitting in an office. I felt like saying, "Shovelling shit in the dead of winter or sitting in a nice warm office on treble the money? Tough one," but I resisted. Instead, I told him that I'd worked at a friend's recruitment business helping out for a few weeks, and found I really enjoyed it. But now it was time to build a career, and having an affinity for sales, recruitment seemed a natural choice. I then said, "Give me this opportunity, and within a couple of months I'll be one of your top earners." I was showing him my competitive side, that I was hungry to earn money. He hired me on the spot. It goes to show how important it is to prepare.

None of us are perfect though, and my first day didn't go quite so well. I decided to take the bus to the office and worked out all the times the night before, believing I had left more than enough time to get there. First, the bus was late, then when it finally came, it soon got stuck in gridlocked London traffic. So bad it was, the driver even pulled out a newspaper and started reading it. I was going to be very late for my first day. Never a good thing. I phoned them, apologised profusely, and explained that I was stuck in a traffic jam. Fortunately, it wasn't held against me, and when I got there I hadn't really missed much. I quickly found that it was a different working environment to what I was used to - sitting in a working office environment, people all around me, headsets on making sure they were always on the phone. It was all about minutes; if you didn't have enough sales and phone minutes, you were out.

I settled into my new role over the next few days and asked Amy to take up some of the slack for the next few months. I was determined to make an impression, and immediately set about doing so. When I got home I was straight into my home office, working on my business. It was definitely flat-out.

Though my new job wasn't the same as running my own business, it had parallels. I loved the feeling when I finally got someone into work. Hearing the excitement over the phone in their voice because you have just got them a job; or pushing that client who was only looking for two workers to getting him to take five. It wasn't the same as my business, because I was only getting companies to advertise jobs on my website and making sure they had plenty of applications for each one; past that stage I didn't really control any of it. But I would often ask my clients their opinion of the candidates and if they had hired them via my business.

Recruitment is something that I was, and still am, very passionate about. By the end of my first month, I'd broken the company record, getting seventy-five people into work. I had to work extremely hard, and my social life was non-existent. It was a sacrifice I had to make, as it was all about getting that half-million investment, and the meeting for that was getting closer.

That's when my relationship really began to break down with Laura. We became more and more distant and had grown apart. I must shoulder the majority of the blame, as I wasn't giving her enough attention. I was trying my absolute hardest to get success in my business, for us to be financially secure. I thought it would bring us closer, but it didn't, it drove us apart.

We lived right on the banks of a beautiful canal at the time. When I would come home she would still be at work, so I'd take the dog out for a nice walk along the canal, to think about everything.

Strangely, I sometimes missed working on the roads. Having a good laugh with the boys, covered in mud and sweat, getting so physically exhausted and being able to fall asleep as soon as I got home. Now, this was a different kind of tiredness I was feeling. It wasn't my body that was tired. It was my head, constantly spinning. I would have to walk along the canal with the dog to try and switch off or calm my head down for a bit before coming back in and working. Even when I tried to get a few hours' sleep my head just kept churning; it's very hard to switch off.

After one such walk I came home one day and had a chat with Laura about our relationship. We could both see it wasn't working.

She started crying when I tried to kiss her. There was something she wasn't telling me; I asked what it was. Laura said, "I haven't been paying the rent with the money you've been giving me, we have to leave next week."

I was completely shocked. I had left Laura to sort out bills and the rent, I just gave her the money. But she wasn't doing it.

"Where the hell has the money gone Laura!" I yelled. We argued for a long time, and she just said we had to move out, and that maybe it would help us to be apart for a while.

I agreed, and on the day when we had to leave the house I had arranged a removal service to move me into a flat across the other side of London. She had told me she would be moving back in with her auntie, and they would be coming soon to get her stuff. I had to leave to meet the removals company at my new flat, so I tried to kiss her goodbye again, but she wouldn't let me. I told her I loved her and walked out of the house for the final time.

At my new flat my stuff was all over the place. I had a makeshift office area and made the bed up. It was a bit of a mess for a while as I was trying to work for the recruitment agency and keep my business going.

I kept trying to call and text Laura to see how she was, but she never picked up and said she just needed space.

So I buried myself in work again, and for the second month in a row I got the best sales record. The recruitment company I was working for was doing so well they arranged a football match to be played at the MK Dons stadium. I played right back for that game and even managed to score a goal.

One day, I got a phone call from my old landlord. "Hi Dave, it's Gary. I hope you're okay. I know I normally speak and deal with Laura, but I'm just phoning to say I haven't received your rent for last month and you're due again this month." I told him what Laura had told me and that he had asked us to leave. He replied, "That's the first I've heard of that, you haven't missed any payments, just last month's, and this month's is due next week."

I was completely baffled; what the hell was going on? I had an urge to go back to our old house near the canal as he said the keys hadn't been handed in so someone must still be living there.

I had recently bought myself a Mercedes, so I drove round to the old house. I looked through the windows and could still see things in the house. I banged on the door, no answer. So I opened up the rubbish bin - fresh cans of dog food and opened letters addressed to Laura from only a few days before.

I called her, but as always there was no answer. I kept calling and texting saying, "I know you're still living in our house! What the hell is going on?"

The neighbour came out and asked if I was okay. I said, "Have you seen Laura?" She replied, "Yeah, she told me she's going on holiday with her new fella. She said you broke up with her and moved out, and a few days later she moved her new fella in."

My heart felt like it had been completely ripped out of my chest.

She had completely screwed me over.

I later found out that she had been seeing someone for a while and made up the story about the rent to get me out of the house. As soon as I had left, she unpacked the stuff she'd packed in front of me and phoned her fella and got him to come move in with her, in our house. From the money I was giving her for bills she had been putting some aside each month, saving it for having a holiday with this new bloke who had moved in and who had decided it was alright to start sleeping in my bed.

Crushed and heartbroken I turned and walked away from my neighbour without saying anything. The canal I had walked along to clear my head after some busy days was around the corner. So I went for a walk along there to try and get my head around it all.

Laura then phoned me, as I had texted her auntie asking if she had heard from her. Laura started shouting down the phone, "Yes he's moved in! And you have just ruined my holiday now!" She then slammed down the phone and that was the last time I heard from her.

I leaned on a railing and peered into the canal.

I looked down at what I was wearing. Shiny polished shoes, a crisp white shirt and a well-tailored suit. I had fought so hard to try and become one of those people in the suits, yet hadn't realised I had become one. To be honest, it didn't feel nearly as good as I thought it would. I was starting to turn into someone I wasn't. This wasn't Dave from the sewers who shovelled tons of tarmac each day, this was now David, my alter ego, a posh version of me. I was trying so hard to be a Mark Darcy lookalike and a well-spoken businessman; but I had lost who I was. Maybe that was the reason Laura went off with another bloke from Tesco, she liked bad boys who didn't have much going for them. Anyway, I will put the claws away and put that episode to bed.

Back at my flat, I was unpacking my things and found the picture of my dream house that used to hang on my wall; I hadn't seen it for a while, I thought I had lost it. I sat there staring at it for a while, then realised I didn't have to share it with anyone else for it to happen. This was *my* dream, and I remembered my promise to myself, "No one or nothing will stand in my way."

Even a twisted, conniving ex-girlfriend who tried to destroy everything I'd built and made sacrifices for. A girl who had cheated on me with a Tesco worker who stacked the salads. I have nothing against people who do this, just little bastards who like to jump into other people's relationship and rip it apart. Okay, okay the claws are definitely going away this time, I promise.

The next few weeks were extremely hard. I wasn't sleeping and worked a very hard job that was expecting more and more from me, and my own business was getting busier. It was time to knock the job on the head.

I submitted my resignation and was told to come back anytime if I wanted another job. It was a shame as I was doing very well at it. But my business had to come first. Now I just buried myself in my business and put everything else to the back of my mind. One weekend I drove to Sandbanks in Bournemouth, where there are some amazing houses. Football managers and players alike are among some of the famous faces. It was me just dreaming again, but I kept believing that someday I would have my own beautiful home, and no one would ever take it away from me.

Quiet People Have The Loudest Minds

The day then came for my appointment at Hamilton and Bradshaw for the recruitment entrepreneur scheme and the half million pounds of investment. Their offices were in Mayfair, right next to a luxury superyacht showroom. "One step at a time," I thought, "get your house first." Saying this, I remember once I had asked a client who was an extremely wealthy man if he had been on a superyacht before or if he'd considered buying one. He told me, "The happiest days are when you buy it, and when you sell it," so make of that what you will, but some superyachts cost six figures a week just to keep it running.

I opened the door and was immediately greeted by a receptionist who took my coat and showed me to my seat. I had arrived early and was the first one there. It was the most glamorous office I had ever seen. Everything was sparkling clean and very professional, and it was clear that a lot of money had been spent decorating the place, marble absolutely everywhere, which by this point had become the norm. Other people began to arrive. I watched them walk in. They were possibly twice my age and looked very wealthy. That was clear from the suits they were wearing. Armani, Louis Vuitton... I mean my suit wasn't cheap, but it was no five-figure suit. Then you could see the watches, Rolex and Omega.

As the receptionist sat them down next to me, I sat there going over everything in my head. I started to doubt myself and could feel a strong pull to head for the door and leave. But I thought back to all I had achieved so far, all those times when the odds were stacked against me and I came through on top. This could be another one of those times. I started to try and look at the positives I could bring, looking around at the people next to me. Yeah, they were older than me, so what? I'm younger, enthusiastic, hungry, full of fresh ideas.

The Dreamer

Are they really as ambitious as me? Okay, I used to shovel shit for a living, but I'm here going for the same thing as you, pitching my business exactly the same as you are. My silent rant helped the daunting presence of them wither away, and I sat there with my head held high.

They were probably really nice people, but it was just the competitive vicious animal in me trying to fight and win at all costs. At that moment I saw James Caan walk through the reception; he walked up and greeted a few of the people who had arrived, completely missing me.

Then a smartly dressed woman came into the waiting area and called us all in. We walked through the corridors and down to a very grand meeting room. The doors were like an entrance to a venerable house. The meeting table was old, probably oak, all varnished up. The room itself was quite dark, lit only by lights dotted at each place at the table. Then there was a larger chair, like a small throne. I presumed it was for whoever would be holding the meeting.

I went straight to the front, just to the right of the chairs and the television. I wanted to be closest to the front so if I was asked to speak I wouldn't feel everyone's eyes on me. I could forget everyone else in the room and pretend it was just me and the hosts.

Three people then walked in, they were the hosts. They introduced themselves, told us about Hamilton and Bradshaw, what they do, and what they were looking for. Then came the 'so tell us about yourself' part again. As always, for some reason, I was chosen to go first; but this time, it was probably a Godsend. I didn't have to listen to other people and try to compete with what they had to say, or what I like to call 'dick measuring'. I was just going to go for it. I had been taught by Mercedes that short and sweet was the key, interesting factual points. I started a nice elevator pitch and slam-dunked my unique selling points. As I was talking I could see one of the panellists lean forward, with a big smile on his face. Then I cut it short quickly to try and build anticipation.

After I'd finished they asked me some direct questions and I gave my carefully prepared answers. I could tell by their body language that they were very interested.

Then everyone else in the room took their turn to speak and told long stories about what they had done and achieved, and what they wanted to go on to do. I started to worry that maybe I hadn't given enough information. Had I kept it too brief? I saw one of the investors writing on a piece of paper, so I pretended to lean forward to get my drink and snuck a quick look at what he was writing. He wasn't writing anything at all, he was doodling. I had a sip of my water with a slice of lemon floating in it and sat back feeling a smile from inside me.

As each applicant took their turn I started to look for the body language signs. Some were very hard to read, others you could see were clearly bricking it. Their bodies not pointing in the direction that they were talking, minimal eye contact when asked direct questions. Others shifted their weight around their chair, looking very uncomfortable. But some had achieved some remarkable things. "I personally made five million pounds for my previous employer," said one, then another, "I made five and a half million pounds." The classic dick-measuring tactic. Intrigue is your greatest hand; while they were all bragging about what they *had* done. I sat there smug about what I *would* do! It's about the future, not the past.

When everyone had finished, the hosts said it was time to leave and they would be in touch in due course. I walked around the table and made sure I shook hands with all three of the panel and told them I was very grateful for their time, and it had been an invaluable experience just to be invited. I turned my head and could see the rest of the people at the meeting who had made for the door now turn around and copy me. A five-figure suit doesn't get you manners, it seems.

I walked out feeling happy. I knew I had done well. I felt proud of myself. Even if I didn't go any further, I'd have done something

The Dreamer

which would only improve me as a businessman. Gaining confidence and listening to people of greater knowledge and experience had got me through that panel interview. There's absolutely no way I could have done that without the help of those people.

That little business idea that I had scribbled on a piece of paper had just been pitched in a room alongside the likes of others, some of whom had achieved millions of pounds profit for the company that they worked for. They were now looking to go it alone, but I had already achieved that. Don't get intimidated by a five-figure suit and a Rolex, it's what's underneath that counts. By believing in yourself, having that twinkle in your eye that everyone can see.

I had made the absolute most of the few precious minutes I'd had to speak. It made me think back to when I wanted to walk away from it all. I didn't think I could speak like that. If I had quit, then I would never have come to this part of my life - to see the fright of public speaking subside and be replaced by hunger and the fight for success. When people say you can't do something, I say, "Why not?" Anyone can do anything, it's whether they have the dedication to see it through. Keep going, one step at a time. It didn't matter that all those people in that room were in five-figure suits, and from what I assume, very well-educated. They could have all the education and money in the world but were they relentless with their dreams? I was willing to give up everything to make this happen.

You don't have to be perfect to get what you want, just passionate about what you want to achieve, and willing to do whatever is needed to achieve it. You can become successful in whatever you want to do, as long as you keep focused on your end goal.

I had shared a room with people who had lived half of their lives, had letters after their name, had the best education - college, university - then gone into six-figure salary jobs. I didn't even know what an entrepreneur was until I went to one of my first mentoring sessions.

I can't spell or even do my times table. But because I had worked my backside off and had sacrificed my whole life to that point to try to get a better life, I ended up in the same room as those people, sitting amongst them, side by side, competing with them. You have to use the fear, tiredness, sadness, happiness and all your emotions. Channel all of it towards your dream. No one can tell you 'NO' when the person within you is saying 'YES'. Tell yourself that you're not a quitter, that you will never give up, then follow those rules.

Never be intimidated by what people think of you, as it will turn to fear and paralyse you. No matter where you have come from, as long as you can wake up in the morning breathing, you are still in the game. I'm not going to deny that when I first began my journey, I tried to pretend to be someone I wasn't. I wanted to be one of those people sitting next to me in that meeting. But I realised the best person I could possibly be is myself. I always wanted to be the next Richard Branson, but then I'm pretending to be something I'm not. That's the reason I'm continuing to be successful. I'm being me, unashamed of where I have come from or what I've had to go through. I may be this guy who used to work in the sewers, with an accent some might call common, but I'm Dave, and in my heart, I'm a winner. At least that's what I tell myself every day, and so far, it's working.

Your individuality is what makes you unique and special. You can make of it whatever you like, you can change everything in your life at any point. Yes, it's hard, but by God, it's worth it. Don't live your life wanting to be the next someone else; live your life wanting to be you, and have the guts to do it your own way.

Don't let fear stop you doing things that you want to do; fear is the enemy. Imagine what you would do if you weren't afraid of anything.

That success you are looking for might be just outside your comfort zone, so the hell with it, take a chance and try it, what have you got to lose?

It's better to fail at something you love than succeed at something you hate.

But if you don't have the passion and love for what you have chosen to get you your dream, it's not going to work. Make sure you do something you love. I have known people who worked their whole lives in jobs they absolutely couldn't stand, then when they start pushing sixty, they are worried every day they will get laid off, because the job really didn't pay that well and their pension is terrible. But when a vast percentage of your life revolves around that job, don't do it. Don't get comfortable. You get one life, remember that. You don't get a second chance. The time we have on this beautiful planet is ticking away more quickly than you can imagine. I remember asking a lot of old people when I would go to work with my mum what they wished they had done better when they were younger. A lot said they wished they had gone out a hell of a lot more, because they were less mobile now. But even more had told me they wished they had taken a few more risks to try and better themselves rather than settling for second best.

On the way home that evening, I got a phone call from the guy who had leaned forward when I was pitching for the half-million investment. It was literally a few hours after the meeting had ended. He invited me back for a further meeting, where he told me that he was very impressed with my eagerness to prove I had what it takes by going out and getting a job in recruitment. I went back for a few further interviews with him and made it through to the shortlist.

At one of the last meetings, I was told I was someone they were very interested in, but because I had gone to work for that recruitment agency, my commitment to my own business was questioned. Being an honest person, I admitted that it did take a toll on my own business, and it had started to go into decline in profits. However, I had started to build up the applications and jobs again. Fair excuse, but it was too late. I had sown a seed of doubt in their minds. It told me very clearly that I had to be working on my business at all times. The profits for the business had taken a dramatic decline and amounted to only a few thousand pounds a month at one point. I had so much going on that the business really felt the full impact of my not being there.

Unfortunately, I didn't make it any further. I was told that I was too high a risk. I was obviously disappointed but could understand their situation, it was half a million pounds of their money, after all.

I was gracious in defeat and thanked them for every minute they had provided to me, that it had been a fantastic experience. I was told that they would find me a job within Hamilton and Bradshaw if I was interested, but I'd learned my lesson. I politely declined and decided to continue full time with my business.

I phoned Amy and said it was time to get back to it. She was struggling to keep up and look after her kids. It wasn't fair on her to keep leaning on her so much.

The Pinnacle Of My Life

During the next few months I worked my backside off with Amy, getting these applications back up and more job postings. I was going for meetings all over London and one of the best meetings was in the 'Gherkin'; the building is completely covered by bluish glass and looks incredible.

I had an email from Amy saying she had been contacted by an awards company; Next Generation Jobs was nominated for Best New Business 2014. It was a black-tie event with lots of celebrities and 'canapés', a word I later had to google. But it was set for a day when I had three meetings with important clients, so there was no way I could go.

Jason and Aadi were also invited, and I remember getting a very excited phone call: Next Generation Jobs had won Best New Business 2014. I was gutted not to be able to make it, but the Award was kindly accepted on my behalf by Aadi. He did a superb job at telling everyone exactly what my core belief was and what had driven the real success of the business. It truly was an amazing accolade and one that still makes me proud to this day.

Soon after, I received an email from Jason saying that he was looking for people who were seeking growth investment, and he had thought of me. He had some contacts who were looking for investment opportunities and were willing to commit a six-figure sum. Would I be interested? Of course I was. I was delighted that he had thought of me as I was actively looking for investment, but I was running out of alleyways to explore. There was only so much longer I could carry the business without plugging in more capital for the next stage of growth. If I did not grow and expand the company, I would risk losing the client base I already had. I was stuck in a catch-22 situation, and this offer came at the perfect time.

The Pinnacle Of My Life

I had so many ideas and ways to push the boundaries of recruitment, ideas that would revolutionise the way people looked and applied for work. Then I worked on the figures and was pleasantly amazed to find that my company had a value in the six figures. The website had an average earning of around £10,000 each month since I started it. In my best month I earned nearly £25,000. It had dipped a hell of a lot while I was working at the recruitment agency, but it was picking back up and I had forecast next year's profits to be in at least the £30k a month range. An incredible amount, considering its modest beginnings. I then began to work on the presentation that I would give to these potential investors. A major cash injection was something the business needed if it was to move to the next level. I poured all my time and attention into making the presentation perfect. I decided to pitch for a £100,000 investment. This was the amount I would need to get an office. I had found a perfect location in Bank, London. Desks were already set up with computers and a grand MD office for me.

I wanted to hire full-time people to phone clients and candidates alike, then slowly evolve the business into a recruitment agency that prided itself on helping the young get back to work. This would definitely need big money.

It would mean giving away a proportion of my company, but if done right, it would catapult me and my business into rapid expansion.

The presentation was in London. I had everything prepared and was ready to go. I arrived at the meeting point and was taken through to a surprisingly small room which was jam-packed full of people. The investors were seated and came from many different nationalities. Everyone who had been invited to pitch had a poster of themselves on the wall with their photo on it, along with the company name and a paragraph about the business in different languages. It was surreal.

I saw a few other people I knew walk in. Some were other

The Dreamer

Golden Touch mentees from the youth program, but a lot were faces I had never seen before and from different organisations. It was lovely to see the other mentees and hear how their businesses had moved forward. We sat down and I felt I had a bit of an advantage as I had already pitched my business at the Recruitment Entrepreneur event. So I felt quietly confident.

Then people started to stand up and pitch their businesses and my confidence dropped. They were using PowerPoint in their pitches, as was I, but theirs looked far better than mine. I had used a number of its features and spent a lot of time creating each of my slides, but every presentation I watched in that room had one, simple slide per point or topic area, and then moved on to the next with a single click. It wasn't particularly exciting, but it looked good and it looked professional. Mine was very different and I became embarrassed. I had found out that you could make titles come flying in, spin on the page, make statistics grow bigger, graphics change colour. I had gone to town on making my presentation jazzy and I was immediately regretting it.

I asked the person in charge of the tech if there was a remote so I could control when things would appear, and I would try to make it exciting. But the remote was lost and they couldn't find it.

I couldn't change it now. I started my presentation, and to make matters worse, it wasn't working the same way it had when I had rehearsed at home. The animations I had configured started acting like they were on drugs, all flying in at once. I would be speaking about one point and suddenly a sentence about my following point would invade the screen and start flashing, whilst at the same time, changing colours.

My presentation had turned into a theme park attraction which had a life of its own. I tried to stay calm, focused on the points I was making and tried to ignore the crazy light show going on behind me.

Despite the light show, I felt that the actual spoken presentation had gone well. I talked clearly, stuck to my script, and maintained

The Pinnacle Of My Life

eye contact with the investors. There were other people seeking investment in the room, but I didn't let myself get distracted by them. I just kept focused on the investors. The people who counted.

I just kept to the key points and fantastic features we were going to have once we had investment. "Look, forget this behind me. This business is going to be big, and I mean big. We have had a lot of success so far and it's making amazing progress. There is such a huge market for us. I'm going to make it. You can either join in with my journey and rocket launch Next Generation Jobs into outer space, or in a few years you will be reading about Next Generation Jobs in the Financial Times while getting your shoes cleaned, hearing we had just made history. Imagine that feeling, knowing you could have been part of it and you missed out. Let's do this together, let's make history together!"

After the presentation, I did a few filmed interviews, then walked to the back of the room and met with Jason who was also pitching to the investors for more capital for his business. He was looking for five million pounds to start a new arm of his business and had several people interested.

A few people came up to me and told me how much they had enjoyed my story. They'd found it inspiring how far I had come with the business and the journey I had been on. It was then that one investor started talking to me about the opportunity for a £100,000 investment. My heart began racing. I was unbelievably excited that he seemed to genuinely think I was worthy of this investment. If it came off, Next Generation Jobs was going to be taken to the next level.

I took all the details that I needed from the investor and before I knew it a few people wanted to speak with me about investing. Someone wanted to invest a slightly smaller amount of around £50k for less equity in the business. One person even offered to buy the business outright!

As I had only prepared for the meeting by writing down

everything I would need for the next stage and coming to a figure of around £100k, I didn't really commit much to it. But now a lot of people wanted to invest six figures. So I would now have to create an extremely professional business plan to hand to the investor I would choose so they could see the business as it was and what I would do with the money.

It was absolutely crazy. I had built this business up from living on £2 a day and now it was attracting interest from wealthy international business people. It was a wonderful feeling.

After the event, a few investors wanted to take us out for drinks at a nearby wine bar. We walked straight in. An American investor bought seven bottles of Dom Perignon for a table. There were so many of us the table quickly became full of drinks, and we stood next to it. I was hastily given a glass by Jason and he quickly filled it up. "This stuff tastes amazing," I thought, "it's a few hundred pounds a bottle at least." We were all talking in extremely good spirits, and I thanked the American for a taste of the high life with some excellent champagne. "Get used to it son, there's going to be a hell of a lot more toasts and champagne popping for you in the future!"

Around the same time, I was invited to speak at Portcullis House, which is situated next to Parliament. It's a traditional sort of old English building you see for all the parliamentary offices. Getting into the building itself was madness as there was so much security, similar to that at airports. I was asked to deliver a few talks about start-up businesses to aspiring entrepreneurs. So I spoke about motivational drivers and also about my journey and how far I had come. This always seemed to go down well.

There are so many people out there all hoping to make their business a success and they can relate to you in those early stages. I remembered how inspired I had been listening to successful businessmen and women speak at the lectures and workshops of the Start Up Exhibition at Olympia, and now it was my turn to inspire. It was always a good feeling being able to talk about and show how much I had developed Next Generation Jobs. Not in a braggy way, and I don't think it ever came across as such, but to get my message across: If I can do it, anyone can.

A few months later it was that time of the year again; the Start Up Exhibition at Olympia was looming. This year I was attending with my business developed even further. Next Generation Jobs was bigger than ever. I now had the £100,000 investment pending and was feeling like I was on top of the world. I felt I belonged there, that I'd paid my dues. I had been asked to do some speaking at the show as well, which was a great compliment.

Around this time Amy phoned me to give me some devastating news; well, devastating for me, not her. She had been offered a full-time job with a top CEO at a big bank in London. The salary was a hell of a lot better than I was paying her. It was incredibly hard to lose someone who had been with me through the early stages and helped so much. I will always look upon working mums with great awe. The amount of fire they have in their belly is spectacular. Warren Buffet once said, "Wait until women discover they are the slaves of this world." I could never agree more. Amy was the backbone of my business, and losing her made a huge difference, but she was now starting a different journey so I wished her all the best and said she would always have a job with us if she wanted to come back.

She told me the job didn't start for a month as she had to organise childcare, but she was giving me ample warning so I could start to ease her workload before she left.

Amy then suggested I stay at a nice hotel before the Olympia Event. There was only one place I wanted to stay… The Savoy! I asked Amy if she would like to join me for dinner as a thank you, but she politely declined and said she was too busy with her kids and getting ready for her new job.

I was seeing a lovely girl at the time, Carly, who was also a single mum. She'd had a very tough time in the past and managed to fight her way through. So I asked her if she would like to stay with me at the Savoy. She accepted, and Amy sorted out all the details. Amy said, "This is going to be a moment you won't forget, I have really worked my magic here."

The day finally came when I would be going to the Savoy. I was getting ready and put my suit in a suit bag ready to take with me along with a few other clothes. I was going to pick up Carly along the way. Then I had a buzz on my flat's intercom. "Hello?" I said. "Mr Brett? This is your driver, I am ready when you are and can help with any bags you may have."

Who was this?! I never had a driver. "Who organised this?" I thought. I texted Amy asking if she had arranged it. She replied, "Yes, I told you it was a trip you would remember. Make sure you enjoy yourself." I could have cried, that woman really did take care of me.

I walked down to be presented with an extremely well-dressed man standing alongside a shiny black Mercedes S-Class. He came straight over and grabbed my bag then opened the rear passenger door. "Hello Mr Brett, will we be going straight to Carly's house then onto The Savoy or would you like to go anywhere else?" "Just that please," I replied.

I then jumped in the back of the S-Class that was filled with gadgets, while the driver put my bag in the boot.

Coloured LED lights followed the flow of the interior around the car and emitted a nice blueish glow. In front of me was a TV on the back of the headrest. The seats were a beautiful creamy colour, and in the tray by the middle seat there were two champagne glasses and a small bottle of champagne. "Amy has really pulled all the stops out here," I thought to myself; I even had a pillow on the headrest!

We drove round to Carly's and she got exactly the same treatment, door held open while the driver got her bags and I sat in the back with an empty champagne glass ready to hand her. On the journey to the Savoy we popped the champagne open and really enjoyed the splendid features this car had and how comfortable the seats were.

As we got closer, we drove up the same street where I had walked when I came to Olympia two years earlier. Holes in my shoes, a badge holding the crotch of my trousers together and a laptop bag, without a laptop. Now I was driving up the road and just pulling into the main entrance to The Savoy.

Carly looked at me and said, "WOW this place looks amazing!" We pulled around the roundabout and before I could even reach for the door handle, the Savoy doorman in a top hat opened the door for Carly and me. "Welcome to the Savoy Sir," the doorman said. I couldn't help but smile. I reached out and grabbed Carly's hand, then the doorman said, "I will take your luggage to your room Mr Brett. Paul will show you to the reception to check in."

The driver and the doorman then opened the boot and grabbed my things as Carly and I walked through the revolving door and into what can only be described as heaven. Golden chandeliers, black and white marble tiles on the floor... everything was sparkling. Paul then stood graciously by the receptionist with a beaming smile waiting for us to come over. We were just standing there in the middle of the entrance hall looking around at how impeccable everything looked.

We walked over and checked in. Paul the doorman then introduced the receptionist and went back to the main door. As we chatted to the receptionist another extremely well-dressed gentleman appeared next to us, with a charming smile. "So, you will be staying in one of our Royal Suite rooms. The Royal Suite has several rooms but as we have it vacant and you are a very special guest, we have opened up one of the bedrooms for you." Indicating another colleague, Paul continued, "This is Sebastian, he will be your butler for the two nights you are with us and if you need anything please let him know."

What!? Our own butler! No way. Sebastian then introduced

himself and we chatted about how beautiful the hotel was while he walked us to our room. Even in the corridors you can see every detail had been thought of. Golden lamps lined the walls and it just looked amazing.

"So, as my colleague has already said, this is the Royal Suite entrance and it has several rooms each with their own entrance," Sebastian said. We got to the door and he opened it.

WOW! The bed dominated the room that was completely lit by the huge window. Sebastian showed us around the room and I went straight up to the window for a view; you could see the River Thames straight ahead, and to the right, Big Ben and the London Eye. "The views are one of the highlights of this room I personally think," Sebastian said. He was right too. Then he led us around the corner. "This is your bar area, and as requested we have a bottle of Dom Perignon on ice." Amy was still surprising us.

Then he showed us around another corner into one of the biggest bathrooms I have ever seen. A stand-alone bath, a huge shower and a double sink embedded in beautiful marble.

We then heard the doorbell ring - this place even had its own doorbell! Sebastian said, "I will answer that for you Mr Brett, that will be your luggage."

We just stood there in the middle of the bathroom looking around, completely gobsmacked by how dazzling this place looked. You could run your finger along any surface and not find a single speck of dust.

Carly then found a silver pot and opened it. They had even thought of bath salts. A pot full of bath salts, such luxury.

We walked back around to the bar area to be greeted by another gentleman. He introduced himself as the head butler, Sean Davoren. An impeccably dressed and well-spoken gentleman who then made sure we had everything we wanted. "Sebastian, make sure Mr Brett and his partner are well looked after." We turned to look at the bar area where Sebastian had poured two glasses of Dom Perignon and was about to hand them to us.

I can honestly say I don't think I have ever been treated so well in all my life. Every single person we had met and spoken to was extremely nice and couldn't do enough to help.

They all left the room and Sebastion then showed us the phone and a special button that, when pressed, connected us directly to him if we needed anything. He asked if we would like our bags unpacked. We said, "No thank you, I'm sure we will be fine, you have made us very welcome."

He then left and it was all completely silent. We just looked at each other, trying to take in what just happened. We were treated like royalty.

We then started unpacking and explored the room. We found the door that led into the main area for the Royal Suite, but it was locked so we couldn't see inside. If this was one of the bedrooms for the Royal Suite, what would the main area be like? We never got to see inside, which was a bit of a shame, but our room was definitely enough for us. We saw a handwritten card welcoming us to the hotel and some very delicious cakes that looked too nice to eat.

I texted Amy to tell her how nice it was and what a brilliant job she had done. She replied saying I was welcome, and she had made arrangements for us to have dinner in the Savoy Grill at 7.30pm.

Savoy Grill? That's Gordon Ramsay's restaurant. This was the place where Winston Churchill used to dine when in parliament. Now Carley and I were going there. Carly started to panic. "What the hell do I wear?! I'm going to have to find a red dress like Vivian in Pretty Woman." I phoned Sebastian to ask what the dress code was and was told it was just smart casual. It's not designed to be a restaurant of suits and bow ties; they want you to feel comfortable and have a good time.

This calmed Carly down a bit. I suggested we take a dip in the pool. So we donned our Savoy robes and slippers, then walked towards the lift.

The Dreamer

The doors to the golden lift opened and you could see it wasn't just any ordinary lift. The colours were red and gold and there was a big mirror, below which there was a leather chair. This place is just full of surprises.

We went to the swimming pool and were greeted by another receptionist. "Mr Brett, how are you today?" How the hell do all these people know my name, I laughed in my head. It's that attention to detail, I think, that makes this place so special to me.

The pool is surrounded by mirrored windows in a dark wooden frame and just looks so nice.

I leapt in the pool - to hell with it, there was no one else in there! Big splash! Carly was far more elegant and gracious on her entrance than I was. We swam around for a bit, then I saw on the wall, "To operate the Jet Stream press the button below."

What is a jet stream? To hell with it - and I pushed the button. A big rumble followed, and half the swimming pool turned into fast-moving water. The jet of water allowed you to swim against it, so you didn't have to do laps of the pool. You could just keep swimming against the jet stream as long as you wanted.

After a while we got out of the pool, and as soon as we sat down, a lady brought over two towels for us that were lovely and warm and so soft.

We made our way back to the room, and as were getting ready for dinner we played Seal's 'Fly like an eagle' in the background, and it added to the experience. Carly was getting ready in the bedroom, so I decided I wanted to try out the stand-alone bath with the salts. So as Carly was getting ready, I sipped on my Dom Perignon in a bubble bath, reaching over every now and again to get an olive or these cracker things that came with the champagne. Whatever they were, they tasted good.

Just as I was getting ready we heard the doorbell. I opened the door. "Mr Brett, I'm here for your turn-down service, would you like me to come back later?" I was completely baffled at what a turn-down service was and just said, "Sorry love, I don't know what a turn-down service is, I'm a bit new to all this." She then smiled at me and explained what it was. We were just leaving anyway so she went in to get the room ready for when we returned while Carly and I headed down to dinner at the Savoy Grill.

We enjoyed cocktails, wine and what I have to say is by far the best meal I have ever had in my life. I saw caviar on the menu, so like little kids we sat there laughing and saying, "Shall we do it? I'll do it if you want to. If *you* try it I will." I always remember what Jack said in the film Titanic, "No caviar for me thanks, never did like it much." But we thoroughly enjoyed it and had the signature dish for our main, the beef Wellington which was absolutely divine. We could instantly tell how Gordon Ramsay's reputation precedes him with regard to cooking.

We decided to go for a few drinks in the Beaufort bar within the Savoy. We walked down towards the door and met the gentleman outside the bar. "Evening Sir, do you have a reservation?" he asked. "No, we just thought we would come down for a few drinks if that's okay?" I replied. He then said, "Unfortunately Sir we don't have anything available for about an hour." We were gutted, so Carly then said, "Can you call us in our room when a table opens up for us please?" Immediately the gentleman apologised and said, "I am terribly sorry I didn't realise you were guests. We have a table free now for guests at the hotel."

I turned to Carley and said, "He must have thought we were riff-raff off the street." We both laughed and enjoyed another bottle of Dom Perignon at the bar while listening to a wonderful pianist. It just set the mood and setting for a beautiful experience.

Back at the room we saw what a beautiful job the housekeeper had done. 'Turn-down service' was getting the room ready for bed, curtains closed, and the bed opened ready for us to climb in. The radio next to the bed was playing jazz and blues on a low volume, it was Frank Sinatra, Fly Me to the Moon. We really were flying.

The Dreamer

I asked Carly if she wanted a nice breakfast in bed next morning before I left for Olympia. Amy had already texted me to say the driver would be waiting for me outside in the morning to take me to the event. So we knew what time to book breakfast in bed.

We woke up in the morning before our breakfast arrived and, before we knew it, the doorbell rang. In came Sebastian with our breakfast on a massive table. He put it next to the window and we enjoyed a delicious breakfast while watching London wake up.

I got my suit on, kissed Carly goodbye and walked down to the entrance of the Savoy where the S-Class Mercedes was already waiting for me. The doorman opened the back of the Mercedes and I jumped in. A glass of freshly squeezed orange was sitting in the middle tray waiting for me. The driver then set off for Olympia.

As we approached, it brought back so many memories. Standing in the queue waiting to go in, with just a dream. Now I was living it.

We pulled up outside and the driver said he would open my door. I got out and saw everyone in the queue waiting to go in. Jason was already waiting for me and said, "Come this way, straight in." I walked past the front of the queue and was allowed straight in. Some people were already inside, but the queue was so big, they couldn't let everybody in at once.

I walked directly over to The Golden Touch, strutting my stuff, waving away all the salespeople whom I'd let plaster me with leaflets and sales talk last time. I was no longer that easy target.

I looked for Mercedes and I saw she was on the stage, microphone in hand, wearing a very sharp suit. Mercedes had very much acquired her own particular style, something else which I admired her for.

The Golden Touch had set up another Dragons' Den investment platform. I then looked at the panel and saw a few familiar faces from a couple of years before. I saw Aadi too, and he caught my eye and gave me a big thumbs-up and a wave. Everyone turned to look at me, which, I must admit, felt rather good. I suddenly felt important, someone of worth, not just someone who walked in off the streets in a hastily repaired, poor quality outfit, like me, two years before.

I watched on as the entrepreneurs were completely grilled on stage in front of everyone. Then there was a quick break and I thought I had best look for Mercedes and Jason, but before I could even look around, Mercedes came from behind, grabbed me, and exclaimed, "Are you ready to go?"

I looked at the crowd of people sitting there, there were hundreds of people. It was definitely the biggest group of people I had ever spoken in front of.

Then along came another of her pep talks. Don't ask me how she does it because I have no idea. I could have sat there for weeks and still not been ready, but suddenly I was up and raring to go.

Mercedes began addressing the crowd. Everyone sat down, and even more people tried to cram around the area because she was really engaging everyone. Mercedes gave a short talk, getting everyone excited and full of anticipation, then I saw her hand pointing in my direction as she said, "This person has been through startup funding and built his company into an award-winning business in the space of two years having had no previous experience whatsoever. He has also just received ONE...... HUNDRED.........THOUSAND pounds investment to grow his business. Please welcome on stage our David Brett."

There was a big round of applause as I walked on. I stood there at the podium, microphone in front of me, waiting for the applause to stop. I smiled and slowly looked around at the crowd all eager to hear what I had to say. Then silence. "What do I start with?" I thought to myself. So I began the story about how I started, and then went onto the investment I had just got, then ended with, "You know what, I stood at the back of this room two years ago. Too frightened to come near the front because I might be asked to say or do something. It could be you standing here in a couple of years too, all you have to do is believe in yourselves. Believe in your idea.

The Dreamer

"If someone who used to shovel tons of tarmac from a boiling lorry, or clean up other people's waste in the sewers can do it, then so can you! Just do it step by step. One step at a time is not too difficult. Aim for the stars and even if you reach the clouds you are still higher than when you started.

"I have met some fantastic women along my business journey. Mercedes, my business mentor, has guided me along the route and I wouldn't be standing here as confident as I am without her. Amy my assistant, and backbone, a stay-at-home mum who has worked her backside off for my business while also looking after two children is something I will always be incredibly grateful for. The dawn of a new era is coming for women. Just over a hundred years ago women couldn't vote, nor could they use a toilet while out shopping, they had to go home. Now look, powerful women absolutely everywhere. Your sex doesn't define your destiny anymore, you are free to achieve the ultimate success in whatever you wish to do, show the whole world what women are capable of.

"Everybody - learn from absolutely everything you can, there's nothing wrong with standing on the shoulders of geniuses, it just means you can see a little bit further than they can. You never fail in life, everything is just a lesson. As I look back on my life, I see that every time I thought I was being rejected, I was actually being re-directed into something better. Life doesn't come with instructions, there is no set path for any of us; and always remember, none of us is going to make it off this beautiful planet alive. It's up to you to be the best you can be in the time you have. Make sure you are like a freight train in life, make sure you are unstoppable. Now, good luck everyone, in whatever it is you are trying to achieve. And remember, be unstoppable!"

I put my hands up to say thank you and before I could finish and say it, the whole crowd stood up from their seats and started clapping. I waved, then clapped back at everyone else mouthing 'thank you' to the crowd, as by this point they wouldn't be able to

The Pinnacle Of My Life

hear me over the clapping and whistles.

As soon as I walked down from the stage I had people coming up to me, handing me their business cards, telling me we should work together. It was a very odd experience. It had always been me chasing everyone else for their attention, but now they were chasing me to get mine.

As the day drew to a close, I began to want more of the feeling I had when I was up on the stage. I had hated public speaking before. Now I felt like I missed it and wanted to keep doing it. I wanted to help people believe. As many as I possibly could. I wouldn't even want to guess how many hands I shook that day and how many people I met. It was a very memorable experience.

The first day ended and I phoned the driver to come and collect me to go back to the Savoy and see Carly who was enjoying a little spa day in the hotel.

I arrived at the hotel and we decided to get some dinner and have an early night.

The next morning we had breakfast, packed our bags and checked out. The Savoy hotel was incredible and I feel everyone should experience it at least once in their life. We were treated like royalty the whole time.

The driver dropped me off at Olympia for the second day, then took Carly and our bags back to her house.

I went back into Olympia, not to speak but just to see everyone again. It was around late midday at this point and the crowds that came in the morning had slowly started to dwindle. I met up with all the Golden Touch staff, mentees and investors.

After the show, a few of us decided to celebrate with a night out in London. The millionaire mentors showed us parts of London that I didn't know existed, and we were taken to some seriously posh bars where we were treated like celebrities. We jumped queues, had our own tables and private booths. In one place, a private booth cost over £1,400 just to have it for a few hours. Madness. We drank

The Dreamer

champagne, swapped stories and laughed late into the night.

Shortly after that, I was asked to attend a party for Jason's new project he was launching and for which he'd just received millions of pounds in investment. The event was at London City Hall, and I went along in my flash suit as always. It's a very sophisticated place, and to get to the basement you have to walk down a long, circular slope from where there's a view of everything that is going on below, so I could see that there were many people I had met before - mentors, mentees and some investors.

Before, I would have stayed in the corner, avoiding speaking to people, nervous to speak with them. But not now.

It took forever to cross the room; so many people were stopping me, talking to me, asking about my business, trying to sell me their services. It was a fantastic feeling.

I drank some of the very nice red wine. In fact, I drank a lot of the very nice red wine. A bit too much probably. Then Jason came up to me and asked if I was okay to do a little talk. I could hardly say no, I just wished I hadn't drunk so much. I loved public speaking by this point.

I went up on stage and gave my usual speech, followed by my plans for the next year - the London-based office, the expansion, the team, the investment. It was very well received and I got a huge round of applause. When I walked off stage, people began shouting things like 'GO ON DAVE!' People were being so nice.

I was then interviewed, half-drunk, by a lovely young lady. Everyone just seemed so intrigued by my business adventure. To be honest, every time I spoke about what I had gone through so far, even I had trouble believing it. But here I was, presenting to half of England's capital city on a business that I owned. I even managed to meet the future Prime Minister Boris Johnson, who had walked over to see what was going on. We all know he loves a party.

After the event finished I literally put all my eggs in one basket and put everything into this investment. I went up to London for meetings with my investor and went over all the paperwork; it was the most exciting time of my life.

I went to see what would be my new office in Bank. It was a beautiful workspace. Each desk had a phone and computer.

When I started, I didn't even have a computer, and my phone rarely had any credit on it.

I walked around it and it felt perfect. I imagined what it was going to be like, hearing my staff phoning businesses saying, "Hi, this is Next Generation Jobs." God, it felt good.

Stars Can't Shine Without Darkness

One day I opened a brown envelope with my name on it. It was from the tax man, and he wanted his share of my success. I hadn't thought about this. I then had to find an accountant to do my tax return for the business and was then told they had been chasing me for a long time and only just found out where I lived. As such I had piled up mountains of late fees and penalties. The tax bill was absolutely huge. To the point I didn't even know if I could pay it. I had just put a huge deposit down for this office and poured the rest into getting the next phase ready. I completely forgot about paying taxes, it just wasn't something I remembered, I always had so much going on each day. Amy was now gone and enjoying a successful career, so I couldn't ask her to look into it or sort it out anymore.

I couldn't tell Jason or Mercedes about it; it would make me look stupid. I was on my own.

I didn't have much of a choice. I had to tell my investor about the tax bill. I tried to call him but couldn't get in contact. Then I sent him an email. I received an email back from the investor's assistant.

I suddenly lost all contact from the investor. He wasn't replying to emails, phone calls or texts. He obviously didn't want to know anymore. I was so close, we had done all of the paperwork, everything was done and ready, all that was left was the final signature and then the transfer of the money.

I was heartbroken. I was embarrassed. I was angry. I had told people I was going to be receiving this investment. If I got it, I could pay this tax bill and have some left to try and keep the business going. I was even recruiting for staff, including being in the process of employing a receptionist. Everyone had heard about the investment coming my way. I had put together the business plans, the forecasts; the business could be turning over millions within the next few years.

I remember being at that very first Start Up Exhibition at Olympia, standing at the back of the audience watching the huge stage; the people pitching their ideas, being asked how much would the business be making in the first year… and it had scared me. I had thought, "How would anyone know that?" I knew now. I knew exactly how much my business looked to make in the next year, and the year after that and the year after that. In fact, based on its growth over the past twelve months, I had a pretty good idea of what it would be making in five years.

I had done all of the work, the calculations, the grafting. And they knew it was possible. They knew it could happen. That's why I had been offered and promised the £100,000 investment. We were ready to go. After wasting the first £5,000 grant, I had re-started with my friend's loan of £1,000 and I had worked my arse off to create and grow a business that was valued at £400,000 within the space of a few years. That was all my own work. Imagine what I could do with £100,000, and an office full of salespeople.

I tried to put on a brave face, but behind it, my world was disintegrating. I was still trying to work on the business, but suddenly it felt like the tide had turned, and now everything was working against me. I was exhausted, mentally and physically. I had been fighting so hard for so long to achieve my dream, and yet again it was on the cusp, only to have its legs snatched away from beneath it.

I lost all motivation and confidence within myself. I neglected the business and it was just left to fall apart. I felt it wouldn't be long till HMRC took whatever money I had in the bank and left me in the red again, unable to even withdraw £10. It's funny how fast word starts to get around when you're in trouble. The phone calls, emails, texting - all stopped. I was on my own, the mass following of people I had around me had now suddenly disappeared. I lay in bed, not eating, for days on end, wondering why, however hard I tried, something would come along and knock me all the way back down to the bottom. I told Carly I would be busy for a few weeks and wouldn't be able to see or speak to her. She was such a lovely girl, she said "Okay," completely unaware of how bad everything was.

My life continued its downward spiral. I started having trouble sleeping, so I turned to drink as a way to help. Soon I was drinking a lot, every day. The more I drank the more the pain went away, the more I didn't feel like a failure. I could not face people; I didn't want to talk to anyone. I hid away for weeks. I even phoned my mum and asked if I could stay with her in Margate for a while to try and clear my head. I would be so drunk sometimes that I would walk from the house in the early hours, down towards the beach.

I had a bottle of drink in my hands with my hair a mess and my clothes stinking. I had let myself go completely. I stood by a pedestrian bridge looking out to sea, thinking of the embarrassment. It was a very high bridge between two cliffs. I looked down towards the black peril. I leaned over a few times, thinking this would just end it all now. If I fell down I wouldn't have to face the tax man nor the humiliation of people laughing at me. I went there a few times, deliberating whether to just end it all. Most of the time I just cried my eyes out and carried on chugging the bottle of whatever alcohol I had.

It's a horrible place to be, it's like you have no escape. You don't want to talk to anyone or have anyone try to tell you it's going to be okay; you just want to have it all go away.

Would it surprise you if I told you that the highest form of death for young people is suicide? I think there is so much pressure on young people to perform, it's just too much. That means people are more likely to take their own life than to be killed in a car crash or from diseases.

Young people are expected to rise up through such hard starts to life. You are expected to start life on the national minimum wage, which decreases the younger you are. Yet at the same time, the young are charged a premium for car insurance. My first year's car insurance was £3,000. You're also expected to be able to pay unbelievable amounts of monthly rent. I would love to know how you can save for a mortgage when you earn £1,000 a month, and your bills and cost of living are £1,050 a month. The way the system is set up for young people in the UK is crazy. I think the government is so out of touch with the youth of today, that if they were to be put in some of the predicaments I have seen some young people in, there would be a lot of changes in the law. I have seen so much creativity and passion from so many; if they were just given a chance to shine and make some kind of mark on the UK it would be a much better place.

Young parents who want to go out to work are literally working to pay for their childcare. Many are better off staying at home on benefits than going back to work, unless you have a highly paid job. I have met so many young people in the UK who are full of potential for future success, if only they would be given a bit of slack to really stretch their legs.

I was now one of those young struggling people. I was at absolute rock bottom, not wanting to live anymore, turning to drink to stop the pain. I didn't have anything left and I had lost the fight within me. It's like that analogy - it can take days, even weeks to climb a mountain, but if you slip, seconds to fall to the ground. Depression is a dark and horrible place. All the things I hadn't dealt with properly - like splitting up with Laura and other knockbacks - I had just put to the back of my mind and had tried to forget; but now all came back to haunt me. I had become obsessed with success and wanted to be a millionaire before I was thirty, rather than trying to build up the company gradually. I wanted it then and there. I wanted to see the headline, "From sewage worker to millionaire, all before he's even thirty!" The thing that hurt the most was that it very nearly happened!

My state of alcohol-fuelled stupor and depression continued for a few more weeks. Then one day I was browsing Facebook. I scrolled down my newsfeed and saw a picture of this girl. She was my cousin's daughter. There was a picture of her lying in a hospital bed, a big smile on her face, with her two thumbs up. I was aware that she had been diagnosed with leukaemia, but this one picture really captured my attention.

I sat there and looked through her other pictures, her beautiful smile in each one.

It was as if a thunderbolt hit me between my eyes. How can I be moaning and complaining about my life when this beautiful girl is in hospital, not complaining or embarrassed? She had lost her hair but was still glowing with beauty. I thought if this girl can fight like that, then what right have I got to complain?

Some people don't get a chance to push a reset button, as much as some people deserve to. But others are quite lucky. I thought myself rather fortunate, because although I had lost everything that I had been working so hard for I was still going to wake up in the morning, the sun shining, my heart still beating. It was a moment of epiphany.

"Stop wallowing in your own self-pity," I told myself. "I can pull myself out of this mess."

However hard you have it in life, someone will always be worse off than you.

I was a very broken man at that point in my life. I would put on a brave face every day, but inside, my walls were still smashed to bits. At least now I was slowly starting to rebuild them.

I went back to my flat, turned on my computer and began to face the music.

I remembered one of the investors at the event I went to who had offered to buy my business. I managed to find his business card and contacted him to meet up. He was an ex-army officer who had done very well for himself since leaving the forces. I sorted my hair out and went down to meet him at a posh restaurant in London. We had a chat about what had happened and where Next Generation Jobs was now. He said he would still be interested in buying my business, as he was creating a company that helped young people who did not want to go to university to get trained and into employment. That meant Next Generation Jobs would be no more and be folded into his company. I didn't really have any choice, so we haggled over a price for the business and I walked away with a six-figure sum. It wasn't the million I was dreaming of, but I could pay the tax man and have some left to maybe buy a cheap house. But what next? What would I do now?

Within that year my mum was rushed to hospital again. I'd saved a bit of money, so when she recovered I decided to treat her to that holiday I'd said I would. I had plenty of time on my hands, and I took her to Mexico to swim with the dolphins. It wasn't first-class flying Emirates to the Maldives like I always dreamed of, but that's definitely something I will do, just not yet. She loved it, and to see her smile when she was amidst a small pod of dolphins made it all worth it. I also got us tickets to see The Nutcracker at the Royal Opera House one Christmas, where she saw David Walliams in the audience. As he came our way she got us both so nerve-wracked and starstruck we both waved insistently. David, if you ever read this book, I'm sorry. I know you just stared at us for a while, grinned and walked off. But we aren't crazy, I promise.

I also booked a trip to Las Vegas with some friends. We went out for a week and had some amazing times, seeing the Grand Canyon and all the other pleasures around that part of the States. On the last night out there two of us had booked a night flight on a helicopter. I sat there on the runway. The engines started and the blades began to rotate. We'd been given headsets, and suddenly 'Mr. Brightside' by The Killers was blasting through my ears. The helicopter lifted a few feet and flew over the runway, and I started getting flashbacks to my time in the flat I'd had in Cliftonville and the bridge where I thought about ending it all. The music still blasting, we heard, "Are you ready, here we go!" Then the helicopter lifted right up in the air and started flying down the Las Vegas Strip.

No matter how bad it is in life, never ever give up. Look to others to give you inspiration when you need it the most, anyone can lie down in defeat. Those memories of ending it all or breaking down completely due to drink were fading and felt almost surreal as I looked out of the helicopter window while we flew over Vegas. It was exhilarating and made me realise that however bad things seem, one step at a time you can get out of that horrible place you find yourself in. No matter how bad it is in life, never, ever, give up. It is part of life to have knockbacks, but it's up to you how you react. Accept defeat or get back up, brush yourself off, and give it another go.

When I got back from Las Vegas, I decided to start putting wheels in motion again. It was a weird kind of feeling. I went back to working on the roads for a bit, this time as a manager, just to keep some money coming in. I had a brilliant relationship going with Carly and once I told her about it all she was incredibly supportive. We bought a beautiful home together and it wasn't like the one in the picture on the wall I had dreamed of... it was better. She made our house a home and it felt so good. Life was on the up.

But I had become very comfortable on my stepping stone. I had set up camp and had been enjoying my responsibility-free life without a business. But, deep inside me, a little voice nagged away. I had to accept it. I did want more.

The setback I had was merely a pause to catch my breath, ready for another go. That's a lesson for you all, never chuck in the towel, you don't know what's right in front of you. Your success could be right on the other side of those walls if you keep smashing them down.

Yes, I have had times when I felt that all was lost and what's the point in carrying on, but I was so naïve, I couldn't see past it all. Things are put in front of us in life to test us, to make us stronger.

You may feel weak at the time, but remember, this is shaping you for the future, this is what makes you mentally strong.

Time is one of the most precious things on this earth; everything that has a beginning has an end. We can't choose how that end comes about, but we CAN choose what we do with that precious time we are given on this earth. Some people like to spend their time in fear, fear of leaving that dead-end job they have been in for years because leaving would be entering the unknown. Don't let yourself fall into that trap. Life is a ticking clock; do not do something you hate for your whole life.

If you want to do something, go and do it, do not let anyone else's opinion stop you from becoming what you want to be. Then when you are really low and feel you can't go on with this pain, find something or somewhere that is beautiful to you, and embrace it. I used to love walks along the seafront when times got tough; I would walk along the beach looking out to sea and think about how pretty everything really is. You really do realise there are many reasons to keep getting up in the morning. You can take everything that life throws at you. There is no shame in failure, and I've learned that the embarrassment and fear soon go away, life really does go on.

You are the strongest of the strong and no one can touch you.

The biggest problem you will have in your life is decision-making, just deciding to get off that autopilot of life and getting out of that cosy existence. Like jumping from under those lovely warm bedsheets and into a cold shower. The most successful people aren't necessarily the most qualified. As often as not it's the people who never gave up, the people who would get up at four in the morning and open the laptop or go to the gym.

Make goals. It could be something small, like to stop hitting that snooze button for a month. Then once you have mastered that, move on to a new challenge. You will start to notice a pride within yourself, the feeling of self-achievement that cannot be compared to anything in life. Facing your fears and conquering them, now that's a goal.

I faced a lot of my fears, not because I had to, I could have stopped and walked away loads of times. Like a lot of other people in this world, we don't like things that push our boundaries, it's in our DNA to play it safe. Once you have pushed yourself that little bit further, you will see it's not as bad as you always thought. I was always so scared of heights that I did not want to go anywhere near anything that involved heights. When I was standing on that bridge I couldn't see the bottom and was too drunk to be afraid. But when I got myself sorted again and went to Las Vegas I pushed myself to go on the glass walk over the Grand Canyon.

One of the things that shaped me into working hard at things was working for my boss who got me the flat when I started my business journey. There was absolutely no way you could go in and have an easy day. He would be on you. I lost track of the days I would go home and would be totally exhausted, with my clothes drenched in sweat. I would strip down to my boxer shorts as soon as I walked in and lie under a fan and pass out for a few hours. I hated it and loved it at the same time. He got the very best out of me. I would go around to his house to pick him up at silly o'clock in the morning. If I was three minutes late, he would be phoning me, asking where I was. I think back on those times now and I thank him for shaping me into a determined person. Every day was a hard challenge, and he would always want more and more from me.

The time to change is never too late, no matter where you are in your life. Just change the route you are going down. It doesn't matter if you're old, young, female, male, rich or poor, black, white or anyone. You have the choice and the time to turn your whole life into something you want it to be. Who knows where you could be next year or even the year after that? It's now a few years after I was at the very bottom of my life, the lowest I had ever been, a broken man. Now you'll find me trying to help anyone who reaches out to me. Life hits you pretty hard and it's always good to have someone in your corner.

I may not have achieved everything I wanted when I started my business, but by God did I make my mark. You may never fail on the scale that I did, but it's impossible to live life without failure unless you live a life of cautiousness, and then you fail due to inactivity. Remember - be UNSTOPPABLE!

The Next Chapter

The next chapter in my life turned a completely different page. I was standing on a building site one day. Then a low-flying jet swished over the top of our site and went vertically into the sky. It was a Eurofighter Typhoon, a British fighter jet.

"I'd love to work on one of those things," I said to the lads on the site. "Nah mate, you gotta be clever to work on one of those, that sort of thing needs proper education, you ain't got none of that mate. You can't even spell!"

Oh yeah? Watch this!

I joined the Royal Navy at thirty years old and became an aircraft engineer, where I'd achieve five GCSEs, A-levels and a degree in Aeronautical Engineering. Don't tell me it can't be done! The greatest feeling in life is doing the things that others have said you can't do.

However, I found you are definitely treated differently when wearing uniform. I found this out when we were going to London to get donations for Poppy Day. We all wore our 1's, this is the best uniform you have. Mine was the uniform you always think of when you think of a sailor.

When we all reached London, we were assigned different stations and given our poppies ready to give to the public. We had a group chat, and as the morning went on someone texted saying they had been spat at, someone else said they had chewing gum stuck on their trousers where someone threw it at them. Then a few hours later, we had people surrounding us shouting all sorts of profanity saying we were baby killers. A police officer came over and told us we should move on and advised that if we fought back, we would be arrested for assault.

We decided to leave the train station and walk around London.

We went into several pubs and were told to leave. "We don't want your sort in here."

Later we went to a place in central London that was set up by the Royal British Legion as a thank you for getting the donations. We all got a beer and a burger, then decided to see if there was a bar that would let us in and have a few drinks. We queued up happy, chatting with each other and laughing with civvies in the queue. Then I saw a man come out, walk up to the doorman and whisper something in his ear. Then the doorman looked at us and shouted, "You lot, Navy, not tonight, we don't want you lot in here."

I turned and walked away. Some of us just decided to call it quits and get an early night in the barracks where we were staying in London. As we were walking back I saw two Army lads, in a closed shop doorway, taking off their 1's uniform and putting on some civilian clothes, then bundling their number 1 uniform in a plastic bag and stuffing it in a hedge. We spoke to them and they said, "We can't get in anywhere, so we just bought these cheap clothes to get a pint."

That's not the London I remember, and it has soured my taste of what I thought was once a great city.

I have never been back to London in uniform since; I don't feel welcome.

As the years go by my time in the Royal Navy will come to an end. Richard Attenborough said, "The time of the green entrepreneur is coming." When I do leave, I think I will start a new business designing ideas good for the environment. I am currently working on a drone that recharges batteries during flight. Don't believe people who say, "Everything has already been thought of." There is always something new to design and invent. I will use the money from this book to make some of the most groundbreaking green inventions anyone has ever seen.

Carly and I ended up staying together. We have a three-year-old daughter. I never thought I could love something as much as I love

The Dreamer

my little girl. I sometimes find myself lying there at night, time-travelling back to all the events of my life, when suddenly two little hands will reach around my neck and give me a big cuddle out of the blue; my daughter cuddling me in her sleep. Then I think, "In all those years of struggle, how could I have known the best parts of my life would be yet to come."

The End

Inspirational Quotes.

"If today was the last day of your life, would you want to do what you are about to do today?" - Steve Jobs

"Success is often achieved by those who don't know that failure is inevitable" - Coco Chanel

"Success is walking from failure to failure with no loss of enthusiasm" - Winston Churchill

"You miss 100% of the shots you don't take" - Wayne Gretzky

"There are so many people that have lived and died before you. You will never have a new problem; you're not going to ever have a new problem. Somebody wrote the answer down in a book somewhere" - Will Smith

"I never failed, I just simply came back down that hill of life to get a better run up" - Dave Brett

Printed in Great Britain
by Amazon